BOOK MARKETING:
The Funnel Factor
Including 100 Media Pitches

* * *

ISBN 978-0-9968972-7-3

***

Editor:
Divya Lavanya M.

***

Cover Picture Credit/Copyright Attributions:
Books: Public Domain Pictures Source: pixabay.com
Female novelist: Peter Bernik/Shutterstock
Doodle set of arrows: MinaRim/Shutterstock
Black Leather Texture by inxti/Shutterstock

***

Published by Educ-Easy Books
via CreateSpace
www.GiselaHausmann.com

"In a world where media attention is the coin of the realm, the Funnel Factor gives actionable advice on getting your book the favorable notice it deserves. "
— Phil Yanov, Founder, Tech after Five

"This book, by a veteran writer, offers a treasure trove of helpful pointers to writers-especially on self-published books-on finding markets for their books and getting the maximum attention. The material is practical with guidelines on how to make the tips/action steps work best. One of the most useful sections cover 100 media pitches covering print, television, and radio. Dealing with libraries is also well detailed. Key chapters elaborate on free marketing via blogging and Twitter promotions; monitoring your books' coverage in media and at libraries; making use of writer's groups and social media platforms; and various writing-related organizations and outlets. Many relevant websites are provided. "
Judge, 25th Annual Writer's Digest Self-Published Book Awards

"Impressively informed and informative, and thoroughly 'user friendly' in organization and presentation, "Book Marketing: The Funnel Factor" will prove a practical and invaluable instruction guide and manual, making it unreservedly recommended for self-published or small press author in the process of building an effective and efficient marketing plan for their book."
— Jim Cox, Editor-in-Chief, Midwest Book Review

CONTENT

The Funnel Factor in the Olden Days

All of us decide to write and publish for different reasons. My own journey was quite remarkable.

In 1987, I began dating Austria's foremost aerial photographer; he had taken aerials of all but two of Austria's Fortune 100 companies and hundreds of smaller companies' headquarters and factories. In early 1988, he got into a discussion with the mayor of Vienna about how to portray Vienna best. Florian told the mayor that only the most awesome, beautiful aerial photography coffee-table book could do the city's beauty justice; no single picture could ever do, only a collection would.

When Florian came home, he and I discussed the topic. An avid book lover and collector of coffee-table books, I made a few suggestions about how such a book should look like. Already a few days later, we met with an Austrian publisher who was eager to hear our ideas.

The discussion went back and forth. In the end, a potential collaboration never materialized, because the publisher argued that our book should not have a laminated, four-color slipcase. It would be too expensive.

Regardless, in the meantime, Florian and I had set our mind on that we could and would publish this book. Even though none of us had published even only a paperback book, we pressed forward with the production of a hard-cover coffee-table book with a laminated, four-color slipcase.

Florian had 21-years of industry experience shooting aerial photography pictures; his best friend was a small publisher of art books who could help with advice. And, after hearing my suggestions, Florian was convinced that I could design an awesome book.

Additionally, Florian also knew the market for this book; he assumed that the owners of the companies who had bought aerial pictures of their own factories were also going to buy this book.

Our plan was a plan. We learned everything about lithography, off-set printing, and book binding.

Eight months later, in November 1988, we released "VIENNA – Aerial Panorama."

Just as Florian had predicted, the owners of the businesses who had bought his pictures also bought the book, for themselves and as a gift for business friends and partners. Soon, their employees did too; word spread, slowly but surely.

Even though we had never published a book we knew people who helped us **create a funnel to help sell our book**.

Eight months later, an unannounced visitor came to see me at my office in Vienna. He said, "Hello, I am Paul. I own a bookstore in Atlantic City in the United States. Is it true that you are selling the most beautiful book about Vienna? If so, I'd like to buy ten copies. I have clients who will be interested in buying this book."

In the days before the invention of the Internet, sales funnels were nurtured by word of mouth.

Today, hundreds of media outlets (on and offline) offer indie authors an unlimited number of opportunities to reach and engage with many different audiences, worldwide.

Today, indie authors can create a marketing funnel much faster, even if they did not study marketing in college.

fun·nel
[fuhn-l]

.

to concentrate, channel, or focus

.

to pour through or as if through a funnel

Synonyms: channelize, conduct, direct, channel, siphon

Related Words: concentrate, consolidate, focus

About the Box and the Funnel

It is being said that to succeed you have to think **"outside-the-box."** However, few will tell you that all boxes are getting bigger and that it's much harder to think of ideas outside your specific box.

Take for instance my aerial photography book. It is a fair statement that in 1988 only one photographer, Florian Hausmann, could take these pictures of Vienna. Since flying is expensive, only a photographer who knew the city like the back of his hand could succeed.

Today, this box has gotten bigger. Drones have been invented; lots of photographers take aerials in a cost-efficient way. If they don't know the city like Florian did, they can play around until they shoot the perfect pictures "by chance." In the last thirty days, seventeen books about Vienna got published.

This situation is the same for every genre. Therefore, to succeed, authors need to **"create a funnel"** – to magnetize new followers, readers, and fans who help spread the word, thereby making the funnel bigger and more powerful.

Because of the impact of social media, the last decade has seen an unprecedented rise of the celebrity cult. Aside from traditional celebrities, there are also online celebrities.

Celebrities are being "followed," their books sell like hot cakes, even if they contain no novel idea. When in 2016 one famous member of a celebrity family published a biography that also focused on her efforts to lose weight, her book accumulated more than 200 reviews in less than four weeks, never mind that Amazon carries more than 32,000 books about dieting and losing weight. Such is the power of being a celebrity.

So, how do you become a celebrity? And, how do you create a funnel?

An easy way to plan a marketing funnel is to envision the end goal:

Famous authors get

- interviewed on TV
- quoted in magazines
- invited to write articles and guest blogs

and

- their books can be found in bookstores and in public libraries.

With the exception of "getting your book in brick-and-mortar chain bookstores," all other four goals are "doable" for indie authors.

Naturally, online-marketing is easier to do. You can work in your pajamas with "the world" at your fingertips. *However*, and that's the main problem, at any moment you have to share this online space with thousands of other authors.

An additional problem is that on social media platforms "news" has a way of canceling each other out. Most recently, the news of Carrie Fisher's and Debbie Reynolds's untimely deaths dominated the news. This had to affect indie authors who tried to promote their Sci-Fi novels and romance novels. Certainly, people who like Sci-Fi had feelings about the tragically early passing of Carrie Fisher, and people fifty years and older as well as fans of romance novels were probably affected by Debbie Reynolds's passing. During the last week of December 2016, these groups of potential readers probably did not pay too much attention to promotions of Sci-Fi novels and romance novels.

This is one major reason why creating a funnel that also attracts potential readers on offlline platforms is so important. 57% of Americans *often* get news on TV and 46% of these watch local news. TV has not lost its attraction as a mass media since 1955, when about half of all U.S. households had television sets.

Considering that 46% of people who watch the news on TV like to watch **local news,** every author should try to reach this audience.

Pitching a TV-anchor will take about thirty minutes to one hour. Since most likely the station will offer you a morning slot (not prime time), you will also have to get up early and dress "for the big event."

BUT, you won't have to share that space. Typically, local TV stations do not invite more than three guests per hour. That means that you will have the undivided attention of at least 5,000-10,000 people, even in a smaller city. Though not all of these 5,000-10,000 people will rush to buy your book, many of them will. (More about this topic in this book's chapter about the Nielsen BookScan.)

If you are also connected with local friends, acquaintances, and "movers and shakers in your community" on social media platforms, your posting about your guest appearance on TV will put you on the radar of more people in your region. It is also a first step to becoming a local celebrity.

If you pitch a high-end magazine successfully, you will have the undivided attention of half a million or more people who even paid a few bucks (the price of the magazine) to read this information. The shelf life of magazines is thirty days; they get added to the collections of public libraries, corporate office and home office libraries, which does not include the thousands of people who read magazines at Barnes & Noble bookstores nationwide.

Once you get your book in public libraries, you can post this information on social media platforms, too. Regardless whether your book is in the libraries of the people who see your postings, or not, they see confirmation that your book is "hot." Some of your followers may even request that their libraries acquire your book.

Pursuing activities that increase your reputation is considered "nurturing the funnel."

One of the best side effects of this type of marketing is that you are never looking too salesy because you are not selling your book, you are "selling" the concept that you are somebody others listen to.

This concept should be particularly appealing to authors who don't like to be sales people.

To be successful with creating a funnel requires the following skills set:

1) You need to know as much as possible about your topic. If you are a non-fiction author, your field of expertise is obvious. If you are a romance author, you need to dig into new dating trends as well as learn about dating in the olden days. If you are a Sci-Fi author you should be able to talk about the Roswell incident eloquently and follow up on all UFO sightings. If you are a children's book author, you should follow the latest trends in early childhood education. You never know when an opportunity to pitch the media comes up; when it does, you want to be prepared.

2) Be creative! Opportunities don't present themselves on a golden platter; you need to develop a mind-set that helps you find opportunities.

3) Don't be shy! At least in the early stages, nobody is going to come to you and ask for your opinion. You need to pitch others with your ideas and demonstrate that you are somebody whose opinions are worth listening to.

4) Be disciplined. You will need to follow-up on every opportunity quickly. Journalists have deadlines to meet. If you hesitate to act, somebody else on the other side of the country might pitch the same journalist. If that other person is faster or prepares a better information package, they are going to be featured, not you.

5) Be polite and don't write me-mails! Nobody appreciates emails that sound like diary entries. ("I want this and I want that..."). Regardless whether you communicate with a journalist, a TV-anchor, or a librarian, don't talk about yourself but address the topic, the specific issue, or your book.

6) Don't give up! The fact that your pitch may not have worked for a certain news outlet does not mean it's a bad pitch; it only means that this specific pitch was not right for a specific news outlet. And, the fact that one library was not interested in acquiring your book does not mean that others aren't.

7) Last but not least – Enjoy the ride! Like with everything in life, creating a funnel takes time. But, if you are willing to learn from failures, you will get better quickly. And, how much fun you will have! If you thought it's awesome to hold a paperback copy of your book in your hands, just wait to see how it feels being featured in a magazine, or watching a video of you being a guest on TV.

It is doable!

Let's get started.

How to use this book

The latest research on the forgetting curve shows that within one hour, most of us will forget an average of 50 percent of what we just learned. Within 24 hours, we forget an average of 70 percent of new information and new ideas, and within a week, almost 90 percent.

Even worse, when we have own new thoughts, they cancel each other out. As soon as we come up with a few ideas, in our mind, we sort them by importance. Usually, we do not remember the ideas that seemed less important at the moment but might prove to be the most successful in the long run.

Therefore – as you go along, write down every thought, idea, and hunch, in the back of this book. By the time you finish reading, you will be able to devise a perfect action plan to boost your book's sales.

Hint: Richard Branson's "One tip for 2017" was to write down all thoughts.
https://www.virgin.com/richard-branson/my-one-tip-2017-write-it-down

Creating Unusual Funnels

Lately I heard from three authors who all wanted to use a picture they found on the Internet for their book cover:

- a picture of a very unusual, rare car (posted by a used-cars dealer)
- a picture of some interesting artwork posted by a high-end art gallery
- a personal picture that randomly popped up in the author's Facebook feed

All three authors articulated their regrets that they could not find a similar picture on any stock picture provider's website.

This is not the moment to give up!

A few years earlier, I too found myself in the same situation. When Bill Clinton visited Vienna in 2001 he received a copy of my aerial photography coffee-table book. Though I was not personally present at the event, I had a visual proof – a newspaper article with a picture showing Bill Clinton next to his Lear jet, about to receive the book. The photograph had been taken by a Mr. Erich Reismann, official photographer of WirtschaftsBlatt Medien GmbH, a Viennese business newspaper, which also published the picture. Since the work had been performed "for hire," the newspaper owned the copyright.

I desperately wanted to use this newspaper article in my book *NAKED DETERMINATION*. So, I wrote to WirtschaftsBlatt Medien GmbH a nice email, told them what I wanted to do, that I was in no position to buy the picture, that I was willing to name them as the source of the photograph; and, that I would publish any specific text they wanted me to publish to give them the credit they deserved.

Ten days later, the newspaper granted permission to print the picture. They also sent specific instructions – that I had to mention the name of the photographer *and* the publication next to the picture of the newspaper article; they also provided the exact wording.

I replied that I would be happy to print the exact wording *twice*, once in the credit section at the beginning of the book and also next to the picture as desired, and – of course, I did. I also did not crop out the picture but showed the newspaper's name a third time at the top of the article.

As soon as the book was published, I sent the WirtschaftsBlatt Medien GmbH two signed copies of my book, one for the newspaper's reference library and a personal copy for the lady who had been so helpful with arranging everything.

They helped and made me happy; of course I was going to give them what they wanted, and – more!

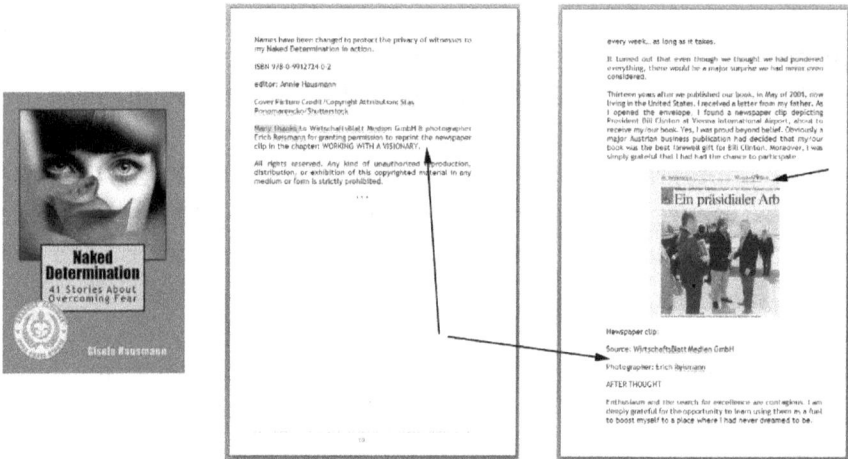

Why am I telling you this now – at the beginning of this book?

I want you to think like that!

There are two ways to go about things in life. You can focus on **problems**

- *"my budget does not allow me to buy this picture"*

or focus on **opportunities**

- *"by giving credit to the picture's owner (the used-cars dealer, the artist, the newspaper), I am introducing them to new audiences." (Logically, if your book never takes off, the copyright owner isn't suffering any losses because nobody gets to see their picture.)*

Obviously, I also could have failed; the newspaper could have declined my offer or not even replied. However, by taking action and writing the email, I could only gain, which is why I am encouraging you to do the same. Never settle for "I can't" but try unusual things to see if they work.

Now assume for a second that the author who wanted the picture of the unusual car had done the same. He could offer to write the following in the front and the back of the book,

> "Many thanks to ...(name of car dealer)..., (city, state)'s first and only premier performance car dealership specializing in sales of hot rods, rat rods, roadsters, street rods, and custom cars. http://**www.xyz-hotrods.com**."

If offered such a "hot deal," more than likely the car dealer would have been happy to provide the picture for free, and he probably would have told all his friends that his car got featured in a book; possibly, he would also have bought copies of the book himself, to give them out as gifts. The author would have nurtured the funnel in an unusual way.

Legal disclaimer:

Most newspapers and magazines have their own specific departments, who are accustomed to handling such issues. If you deal with a small business owner like a used car dealer, an art gallery, or any small business, educate yourself on the Internet on how to word your proposal and offer a straight and fair business deal in which both parties gain something.

Since I am not a lawyer, I cannot give written advice but there are dozens of legal websites that offer templates.

Stay clear of the "Negative Funnel"

Nurturing the funnel is one of the best systems to reach success because everything you do helps channel all your other efforts.

Even if you approach unconventional potential partners like the owner of a rare picture, great things can come from this action step because enthusiasm is contagious.

Beyond that, every successful effort will nurture your *inner* spirit because success drives success. When you feed or nurture the funnel you encourage your "outer" (earnings) and your "inner" development – your skills to find new solutions and your will to succeed.

The same is true for the negative funnel. On every social media platform you will meet people who radiate negative energy. These people only talk about failures, injustice, and compare writing a great book to winning the lottery.

Do not allow these people to funnel their negative energy at you!

Funnels always work, in a positive way and in a negative way.

If you seriously believe that your chances of writing a great book that will sell are the same as winning the lottery, you could also

1. figure out how many hours it will take you to write your book,
2. get a second job and commit to working the same number of hours,
3. save all earnings from this second job,
4. study books about lottery winning systems and strategies, and
5. finally – buy lottery tickets for the full amount.

Obviously, the complainers could do that too, but they prefer to complain; they enjoy creating funnels of negative energy, to justify their own unwillingness to look for new solutions.

Negative funnels are like tornadoes, they destroy and eventually self-destruct.

Positive funnels channel energy toward doing something that will be a positive payoff.

Goodreads

Though this book presents ways to market your book "offline," you should advance your book on Goodreads to boost your efforts and nurture the funnel.

Here is a little secret you have probably never heard before: In contrast to reviews posted on Amazon, reviews posted on Goodreads matter for library purchases.

Though both are online venues, only reviews posted on Goodreads will be integrated automatically into WorldCat, which is a union catalog that itemizes the collections of 72,000 libraries in 170 countries and territories.

More about WorldCat in a later chapter. Here is an illustration showing how reviews posted on Goodreads score on WorldCat where librarians look for books.

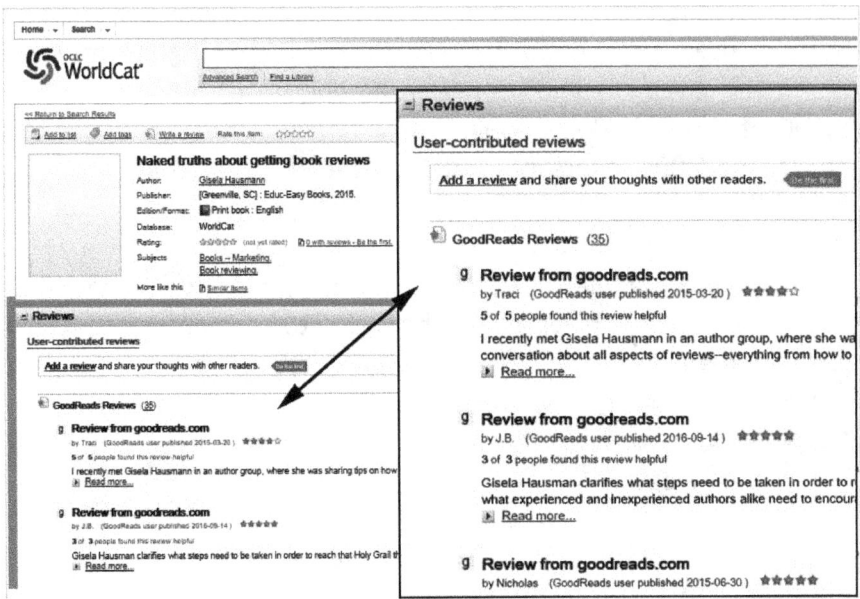

Creating a Funnel on Goodreads

One of the best online platforms to nurture your funnel is Goodreads. However, the often presented statement "... List a giveaway on Goodreads and people will start talking about your book..." is not quite true. If you are already a published author with a large following, this may be true; however, if you are a newbie, most likely it won't.

Goodreads members learn about books when they show up in their newsfeeds. Newsfeeds display book reviews, readers' comments on book reviews *and* give-aways. If 100 people, who have an average of 100 friends each, enter a giveaway, the "news" that they entered the giveaway will show up in the feed of their combined 10,000 friends (100 x 100). Seeing this information in their newsfeed gives the 10,000 friends of the original 100 friends the opportunity to also enter the giveaway. All they need to do is click on the displayed link.

However, in reality, 5,000 of these 10,000 people may not even log into Goodreads for a few days. By the time they log in, the news about the giveaway will be buried among dozens of other news. 3,000 of these 10,000 people may not enjoy reading this book's genre, and 1,000 others may not be attracted by the cover etc.

Additionally, even if 10,000 readers enter a Goodreads give-away, the number of people who can win the book does not change. If an author or publisher gives away 5 books, 5/100 entrants or 5/10,000 will win them.

So, why should you still try to invite as many people as possible to enter your giveaway?

As soon as readers register for your giveaway, your book will be marked as "Want to read" in their "My Books" section (please find it at the top bar of your Goodreads page). That means they can never forget your book unless they unmark it.

TIP: Newer Kindles also show readers' "Want to Read"-lists. Clearly, you want your book right there at readers' fingertips.

With a bit of luck, almost all winners of your giveaway will review your book. That's when it gets interesting. Every time one of the readers who reads your book posts an update about how many pages they read and possibly even adds notes, this information will appear in the newsfeeds of their followers and friends.

TIP: If you know people who read your book, encourage them to post updates on Goodreads.

Naturally, the more often your book shows up in the newsfeeds of readers the more they'll be inclined to read your book because apparently "everybody else" reads it. Additionally, if they click the cover they will see that they already marked it as "Want to read."

Every time one of your friends makes a comment in a **group**, this comment will show up in your newsfeed, as well as in the newsfeeds of all their other friends. That information is important, because it'll tell you who among your friends is active and engaged.

TIP: Try to befriend group members who are active and engaged, and who frequently post updates.

Most importantly, if readers' Goodreads accounts are linked up with Facebook, Twitter, or both, their news updates will show up there too. This is how news about your book will be spread to other social media circles.

In the following illustration, you can see how I marked the progress I made with reading a book, and how this information shows up in my social media feeds at Facebook and Twitter.

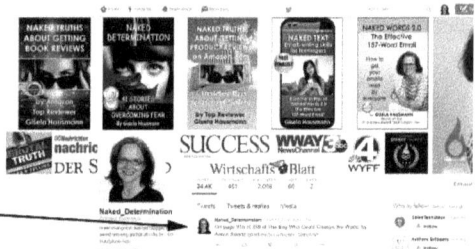

Since early 2016 quite many authors I know disconnected their Goodreads accounts from their social media accounts because they think that Amazon who purchased Goodreads in 2013 collects this data. They believe that Amazon will delete all reviews from people they are connected with. Probably you too have seen postings in Facebook groups that state, "I just lost 70+ reviews. It is ridiculous that Amazon *spies* on my social media friends. I have disconnected all my accounts and I suggest you do too."

Being a top reviewer who reviews a lot of books and products I know that Amazon does not delete all reviews of books from social media acquaintances. I read and review books from people I am connected with; they have not been deleted. However, I do not read and review a disproportionate percentage of books penned by people I know. I read what I like to read and I review most of the books I read.

Since I have no knowledge what other authors are doing I cannot advise whether others should disconnect their accounts or not but I would like to point out one prominent issue.

I have 544 friends and 289 followers on Facebook and 2,212 followers on Twitter. If I would disconnect my accounts my friends and followers would not learn about the books I read.

That's what online networking is all about. In short: Though the people who disconnect their accounts may have reason to doing so, maybe you should not follow their advice to also disconnect. You may be supporting a trend that may cause you to lose opportunities how others learn about your books.

Indeed, there is more you can do on Goodreads to make your giveaway super successful. Of course, it's not all about giving away books but also about hitting a few additional goals.

As a **new author,** you want to make fans who spread the word about you and your work. If you live in the United States or the United Kingdom, you may want to consider approaching your home market first. Maybe you should hold a "1st giveaway" and make your book available only to your home country's readers? You could always hold a "2nd giveaway" four weeks later.

Whereas Facebook groups are very international, on **Goodreads**, you can network with local reader communities including **library book clubs** who focus on specific genres; many of these groups have been established years ago and count quite many members. As examples:

- There is UKYA, a group for readers who like YA fiction written by authors from the *United Kingdom*.
- Similarly, there are the *Texas* Literati.

If you find a group that fits your needs, you might be able to mention your giveaway in the group, thereby increasing the odds to connect with local fans of your genre.

Please note: There are thousands of groups on Goodreads. Each one has its own set of rules. Before you share any information, you must read the group's rules. Ignoring the group's rules can get you banned. On the other hand, excellent effort might pay off big time.

TIP: Since Goodreads does not allow you to contact readers who enter your giveaway, engaging in groups *prior* to holding the giveaway might give you the opportunity to stay in touch with people who know about your giveaway, and maybe even with a winner.

Canadian and Australian authors face a bit of a different situation. Both of these countries are vast and not as densely populated as many parts of the United States and the United Kingdom.

Therefore, Canadian and Australian authors should approach larger or all English speaking markets.

TIP: Before you pick "eligible countries," pack your book exactly like you would when sending it to a winner (e.g. padded envelope), take the packaged book to your post office and enquire about shipping costs. Shipping half-way around the world can be quite expensive. I learned this the hard way when I shipped two books to India. Sadly, neither one of the winners decided to review it even though I spent almost $20.00 per book for shipping; plus, of course I had to pay for the books as well.

TIP: Though in the United States shipping your book via "book rate" is the cheapest option, consider spending a few extra dimes which allows you to include a short letter or a card asking the winner to review your book and also to stay in touch.

If you are an **established author** who wants to break into a specific market, consider doing a giveaway for a specific group of countries or populations, e.g. English-speaking readers in Spain, France, Belgium, and the Netherlands.

Again, to make such an endeavor successful, you will have to take extra steps. Just listing your book and making it available to only readers from these countries is not going to do the trick.

An American author who ignores readers in the US, UK, CA, and AU and selects only other countries will annoy US, UK, and CA readers; at the same time, only very few Spanish, French, Belgian and Dutch people are going to "find" the giveaway.

To avoid such issues, start your giveaway's description by saying something like, "Author xyz wants to introduce herself to English speaking readers in... I will have a second giveaway for readers in US, UK, and CA ... (list date)."

Your goal should be that the people who read your description aren't offended that you excluded them but will be excited to notify their friends in the "selected countries" that there is a specific giveaway — just for them.

Other ways to increase interest in your giveaway:

- inviting your personal contacts (email list)

- networking in Facebook groups

- sharing or promoting on Twitter (paid & unpaid)

- https://www.rafflecopter.com/

- https://www.thunderclap.it/

Lastly, always keep in mind that there are best and worse timelines. For instance, if during December you intend to promote a giveaway on Rafflecopter by offering one to five cool coffee mugs as prizes, this promotion may go very well for you. Even people who don't drink coffee might be interested in participating because they hope that they'll win a mug that they can use as a Christmas gift for a friend.

At the same time, a Thunderclap promotion may be less successful because too many people will ask all their friends to share their messages during the Holiday Season.

Learning on Social Media Platforms – Facebook Groups

Joining various Facebook groups to meet other authors is a great way to learn. Without a doubt it is the easiest way to connect with extremely helpful and knowledgeable people.

It's free, it's fast, and additionally it will help to build up your spirit. Since no success comes easy, you will have bad days, maybe even bad weeks; connecting with others will help you to overcome emotional slumps.

Here a few tricks to get the most out of Facebook networking:

When joining a new Facebook group: Listen and learn before you take action!

1) Check who the real "professionals" are

Members of author groups often conduct surveys, like, for instance, which one of three book covers the other members like best. Whenever you see a posting like this, read every single comment. Some group members will simply state that they like this or that cover; others will explain *why* they like a certain cover. Therefore, these postings reveal other group members' insight, knowledge, and willingness to help.

2) Work on your image!

Make it a rule to contribute to your favorite group at least once every two weeks.

You could post an interesting blog you yourself penned or a blog you noticed on the Internet. You could also present interesting data. Pew Research is only one of the companies that deliver valuable information. Among other great data, they post infor-mation about e-book sales vs. p-book sales, how many people prefer to shop books online vs. people who like to visit brick-and-mortar stores, and similar information that pertains to the industry.

Pew Research has just published its report "Libraries 2016." http://pewrsr.ch/2c507uo

TIP: Before you post, always check the credentials of the blogger or organization so you don't inadvertently post old news from an unqualified blogger.

3) Avoid the cheaters!

Obviously, any author's goal is to sell as many books as possible.

Though there are literally dozens of ways to do this, for instance

> online:
> free social media networking
> paid social media promotions
> features in book blogs
> guest blogging
> articles in online media
> Youtube videos
> Goodreads groups
>
> live events:
> book signings
> networking events
> MeetUp groups
> library events
> media coverage
> private book parties

some authors focus solely on networking in Facebook groups. To be precise, some authors appear to engage in or be interested in participating in some form of review exchanges.

Beware! Amazon does not tolerate review exchanges. When their algorithm identifies people engaging in such activities, Amazon will delete both parties' reviews. All work done by you, like reading the other parties' books in exchange for them reading your book, will be lost, as well as any monies you have invested.

The best way to build up reviews is pursuing at least four to five of the mentioned options so your book receives attention from readers who don't congregate at the same venue.

Take extra efforts to remind buyers at live events to please review your books. It is no secret that the "cheaters," authors who engage in review exchanges, favor e-book purchases. Therefore, you are less likely to lose reviews of paperback books.

Learn About Your Market – Use BookScan

To monitor the results of your funnel marketing strategies, take advantage of the Nielsen BooksScan data.

The US Nielsen BookScan lists sale numbers of "paperback and hardcover copies" by US state and regions within. It is being published weekly. It does not list e-book sales because it was created to help professional buyers. If a book seller does not report to Nielsen (e.g. you yourself selling books at a speaking engagement), sales won't show up in the Nielsen BookScan. Nielsen estimates that they report approximately 85% of all print book sales in the US trade retail market.

Considering how many books are being published today, bookstore buyers and library buyers don't have the time to read blurbs and make judgment calls if and how many copies they should buy based on what they read. Also, fluctuation can be huge.

For instance, in the months preceding a royal wedding, sales of books about royals, weddings, and related topics will climb, but shortly after the wedding they'll fall back to the average sales numbers. After a tragic event like a terrorist attack, books from known antiterrorism experts will climb the sales ranks rapidly, which makes it clear why news and publicity are major influential factors for bookstore buyers.

Of course, there are also trends which are less easy to spot. For instance, a new food trend might emerge in New York City, on the East Coast. Slowly but surely the trend spreads and people begin buying this type of trendy cook book at a steadily increasing rate.

A bookstore buyer from a small city somewhere on the West Coast (far away from New York City) who doesn't cook himself and/or doesn't read articles about emerging food trends won't know about this development.

Then, one day a customer might walk into the bookstore and ask for a cooking book featuring recipes from this new trend.

After taking the order, our fictitious bookstore buyer will look up the Nielsen BookScan. Seeing that the book is selling extremely well on the East Coast, he'll probably not only order the one copy for the customer but also stock a few extra copies.

What does that mean for self publishing indie authors?

If you publish steamy romance novels, which generally speaking most readers read on e-readers, your book's BookScan score may never get high enough for bookstores to stock your book.

If you write reference books for professionals, most likely more people will buy the paperback editions of your book and your book's BookScan score will be higher, automatically.

If you write nonfictions books for authors like I do, the results will be mixed, because authors are used to reading books on e-readers.

Additionally, sales to libraries will show up on BookScan too.

The good news is Amazon shows your book(s)' BookScan results on their Author Central page. Here is one of mine.

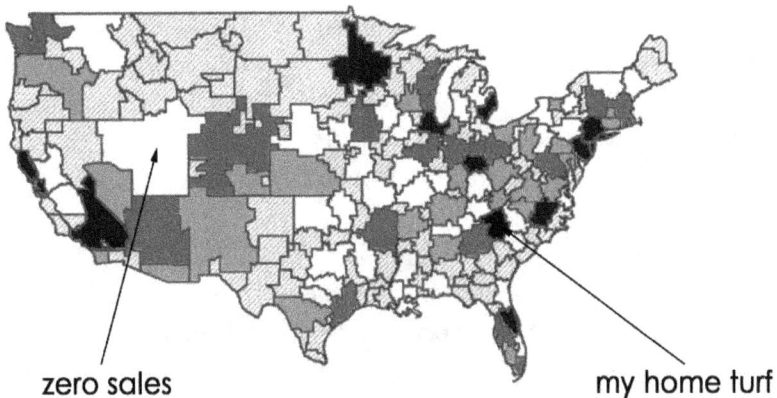

zero sales   my home turf

Though there are hundreds of factors that will influence book sales, this map illustrates an interesting scenario. Looking at this BookScan map, you can see one glaring "white spot on the map," the state of Utah. Considering that people in all other regions of the United States buy physical copies of my books, it seems somewhat surprising that not a single copy has been sold in the relatively large state of Utah.

One explanation might be that my brand is built on publishing naked (no fluff) facts. While surely Utahns appreciate the concept in general, maybe they don't appreciate the titles I chose.

[*Naked* Words, *Naked* Text, *Naked* Truths, *Naked* News...]

As of 2012, more than 60% of Utahns are counted as members of The Church of Jesus Christ of Latter-day Saints. I don't know if they consider my calling my brand "naked" inappropriate. Then again, maybe there is another reason which I just can't guess. In essence, it really doesn't matter but I probably should not advertise or plan a book signing tour in Utah.

TIP: Naturally, you can influence your book's BookScan scores. You can ask your friends nationwide to order your book in bookstores and improve your score this way.

The other way to influence your score is to seek the attention of the media. You can pitch national newspapers, magazines, and TV stations.

That's the route I chose. My book *NAKED WORDS 2.0 The Effective 157-Word Email* got featured in the *SUCCESS* magazine and again in *Entrepreneur.*

If you check the map, you'll see that I sold the most books in regions where lots of entrepreneurs live and work: San Francisco, CA, Los Angeles, CA, Chicago, IL, Detroit, Mi, Minneapolis-St.Paul,

MN, Cincinatti, OH, Orlando, FL, Raleigh-Durham, NC (the Triangle), Philadelphia, PA, and New York, NY.

However, the region where I sold most books is the Greenville, SC region, where I live. This can be explained quite easily: Over the last eight months, I have been a guest on WYFF-4, my local NBC station, five times.

You can also see that I sold books all the way to Atlanta, GA where many Greenville residents have friends and relatives. Probably, quite many people told their friends, "Guess what, I saw this author on TV. She wrote a book about writing best e-mails..." Even being on local TV gets the word out.

People can watch TV or not, but if they watch, they can't scroll away. Equally, people who already spent a few bucks on a magazine probably take the opinions and recommendations of the editors seriously.

Summing it up: Being in the news will get your book into bookstores and libraries; you can monitor the results of your campaigns by checking BookScan, weekly.

Free Marketing & PR – How to Get the Attention of the Media?

Maybe, at this point you'll say, "OK, Gisela Hausmann, you have made you your case. Pitching the media is a great idea. But – I don't know where to start."

Begin by deciding on your greatest strength:

- Do you have a fabulous voice that will make radio and podcast listeners love you?
- Does the camera love you and you love TV?
- Are you a master of the pen, who likes to phrase and re-phrase?

Play into your greatest strength and approach radio hosts, podcast hosts, TV-hosts, newspaper and magazine editors, and top tier bloggers as you see fit.

One of the best resources for authors is HARO (Help-A-Reporter) https://www.helpareporter.com/

If you are not subscribed, you should do so immediately.

- Go to Subscriptions,
- scroll down to
- Sign Up Today and
- "Start Pitching Journalists on topics they want to hear about."

HARO will e-mail you information about what kind of stories journalists, bloggers, other authors, and radio and TV-hosts are working on.

All you need to do is to pitch your angle.

Aside from HARO, you can pitch any editor you like. This is the 21st century, the century of unlimited communication.

- Read as many articles from the media person of your choice as you can. If they are on TV – Watch their shows! Every show has a certain format. Your local news are presented differently than news on CNN. The topics are different and so are the type and the amount of background information guests present.

- Follow your favorite media persons on Twitter

- Share their tweets/material/news (you'll learn a lot about what types of topics are interesting to them.)

- Comment on their articles or blogs

- Don't use a template but communicate in your own words. Most media people have a degree in journalism or related studies. They can spot a template faster than you can say "template."

- Finally, pitch your best idea!

If at times you get frustrated, always remember this marketing method is free. Hiring a publicist doesn't mean that they do all work. You only pay them for making the arrangements; that's all they do. You are the one who needs to write the guest blog, present your story on the radio, or talk the talk on TV. Therefore you might as well contact media people yourself.

***

How to Pitch a TV-Station

The way how you go about contacting any TV station is called pitching. You may be very familiar with the term "elevator pitch"; it is being thrown around all day long.

***

'Elevator Pitch' (definition)

A popular term used to describe the extremely condensed presentation of an idea covering all of its critical aspects.

The name comes from the notion that this "elevator pitch" should be so short that it could delivered in the time period of an elevator ride, typically about 60 seconds.

***

In my personal opinion, elevator pitches are overrated. To me it is just another one of these artificial stress makers, which are supposed to say, "You have to have your act together. If you can't say in 60 seconds what your project is all about, you failed, and whatever you want, is not going to happen."

In contrast, e-mail pitches are much more pleasant to work with – for all involved parties. If the recipients like the pitch, which should be delivered in the subject line, they can take their time to study the whole e-mail in depth; if they don't like it, they can click "delete" much faster than having to wiggle out of a personal meeting; plus, nobody's feelings get hurt.

E-mail pitches give all involved parties the opportunity to be at their best, which helps to achieve a best outcome for all.

It is important to understand that e-mail pitches should still be short and concise, but they don't have to be as short as the sentence a person could deliver in 60 seconds. Additionally, an e-mail can include links or picture attachments.

For more help with writing effective e-mails with personal appeal, please check out my book *Naked Words 2.0: The Effective 157-Word E-mail*.

The Seasonal Pitch

The seasonal pitch is the easiest pitch to deliver. Seasons come and go. If you have lived in your city for a while, you know what is interesting for people living in your area. Seasonal pitches should include a number.

For example,

- "It's time to plant your veggie garden. **3** tips on how to double your crop."
- "The drought in California is getting worse. What vegetables should you plant to save **$25** of your grocery bill every week?"

Both pitches deal with the same topic; the first pitch appeals to local hobby gardeners (local TV), the second pitch relates hobby gardening to an environmental/economical situation (national TV).

The first pitch focuses on "3 tips," the second pitch on "saving $25." (There is the number.)

Other examples:

- Why you should take at least **5** pictures of your mom every Mother's Day! (inspirational)
- Planning your 4th of July party? **3** tricks to do the cooking in half the time! (cooking)
- **7** haunted houses in … (local area) you want to visit this Halloween (ghosts, paranormal)

[Always pick odd numbers (3, 5, or 7)]

Of course, you need to be able to present the answers to these topics and talk about it so viewers will be excited and will want to do what you suggest. Viewers, who are excited about your ideas, will check out what else you did, what kind of books you write. Having seen you on TV – live – makes viewers feel they know you, and therefore they'll be interested in your other works.

The good news is – when you pitch the media, YOU decide what you pitch. Thus, if you can't come up with "7 Haunted House in the area of...," you simply pitch "5 Haunted Houses..." If there are no haunted houses in your area, you can pick something else. The important factor is that you pitch a topic

- which viewers will be interested in learning about
- which also relates to your book, and
- which you can talk about well.

The TV anchors/producers aren't going to criticize your pitch. They only decide whether they like the pitch or not. For them, the only deciding factor is whether your pitch is interesting to their audience. That is why it is easier to pitch local TV stations. You know the audience; they are your friends, your neighbors, your childrens' friends' parents and so on. You also know local customs, and therefore you can tailor your pitch much easier than for national audiences.

Closely related is the Special Holiday or Event Pitch.

The Special Holiday or Event Pitch

Special holidays or events happen on certain days. That means, you have to e-mail your pitch two weeks prior to the event because TV-hosts plan their programs for that event. In other words, opposite to seasonal events, you have to plan your pitch timely.

The nice thing about these pitches is, they return every year, and if you handle your TV appearance well, you can carve out an opportunity for a being a steady guest, again and again. You can become the local "expert," who talks about this topic every year. That is an achievable goal, which will help with selling books even in years to come.

For instance, if you happened to write a historic novel, and you also live in Georgia, you can pitch your local TV station every year shortly before Margaret Mitchell's birthday (November 8) and other dates which relate to Margaret Mitchell and *Gone with the Wind*.

- The **85th** Anniversary of the publication of *Gone With the Wind* is coming up (June 10, 2021). Why are people still fascinated with historic novels about the South and will always be!

Please notice the number – **85th** anniversary.

What if you don't live in Georgia?

You still do the same. Margaret Mitchell's birthday is her birthday all over the world, and so is the anniversary of the publication of *Gone With the Wind*.

The birth of Princess Charlotte in 2015 was an opportunity to pitch

- **5** books parents should read to their child to prepare him/her for the arrival of a new sibling
- **3** beautiful princess story books for all toddlers, not only for real princesses
- Do you know the **3** best princes and princesses story books of all times?

If you wrote a horror novel or a sci-fi novel, you are probably cringing and feeling discriminated. Seemingly the whole world turns around little babies, especially royal babies.

Not entirely...

Horror book authors and sci-fi authors are actually better off. Both can pitch the media every single year, whereas not every year a royal baby is born. Horror authors can take advantage of Halloween and Frankenstein Day (August 30). Sci-fi authors can pitch the media every year shortly before July 8, the day on which the Roswell incident gets commemorated. Also, Star Wars Day is on May 4.

Does your book have something to do with computers?

- *Clean out Your Computer Day* is on the second Monday in February.
- Apple was founded on April 1, 1976, was incorporated as Apple Computer, Inc. on January 3, 1977, and was renamed as Apple Inc. on January 9, 2007 (that's three anniversary dates for Apple, not including the anniversaries of Steve Jobs' birthday and the day he passed).
- The IBM Personal Computer's anniversary is on August 12 (1981).

Did you write a cook book?

- *National Popcorn Day* is on January 19,
- *Fresh Veggies Day* is on June 16 and,
- *Sidewalk Egg Frying Day* is on July 4.

Maybe your local TV reporter team does not even know these holidays, so what better way to teach them and your local community than by talking about these holidays on air?

Hopefully everybody knows that Martin Luther King Jr.'s birthday is on January 19 (plus, there is Black History Month, which is being celebrated in the US and Canada during the month of February and in the UK in October).

Please look for many more holidays you could use to pitch your topic on this website

http://www.holidayinsights.com/moreholidays/

Pitching TV stations shortly before holidays is relatively easy. You can look up the holiday, research the topic, find an unusual angle and then pitch. Not quite that easy is pitching in connection with current events; however, your chance of succeeding with a great pitch is excellent.

The Current Event Pitch

Since I am news junkie, it is my favorite pitch.

I once pitched a TV station about a news event involving Brad Pitt. I know you are raising your eyebrows right now because you can't imagine that I know Brad Pitt. And – I don't.

However, that does not mean that I could not pitch a topic related to Brad Pitt.

In early 2013, Brad Pitt, who had played Heinrich Harrer in the movie *Seven Years in Tibet*, had tweeted on the Chinese version of Twitter that he wanted to visit China. But Pitt was banned from entering China because of his starring role in that movie, which the Chinese government did not appreciate as much as the American viewers.

How did all this relate to me?

In my book *Naked Determination*, I tell the story of how I had met the real Heinrich Harrer, who was Austrian like I am, and how Harrer personally had encouraged me to visit Tibet.

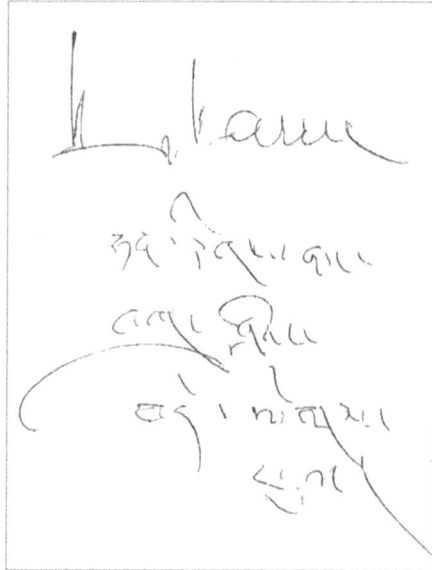

[This is the dedication Harrer penned into my copy of his book *Seven Years in Tibet*; it was shown on TV to add authenticity.]

I had followed Harrer's advice and traveled to Tibet in 1987. I even visited the Dalai Lama's former bedroom, where he and Harrer had many discussions before the Dalai Lama had to flee into exile.

Therefore, my pitch was easy, **"Brad Pitt wants to go to China where is he banned from entering… Local author Gisela Hausmann can explain..."**

[Please note that the current event pitch does not have to include a number because it is not sharing tips but helping to explain a current event.]

If the right pieces fall together, a current event pitch can be that easy to come up with. In this case it was. I had met Harrer, I had traveled Tibet, I had watched the movie, and I was able to *connect the dots*, and therefore – I was the very best and most qualified expert to talk about this specific situation. Probably I could have talked about this topic on national TV because how many people in the US can claim the same expertise and experiences?

Expert authors achieve their status largely by being featured in the media. In this case, I may have been the world's foremost expert on the topic. But, such occasions are rare.

To pitch the current event pitch successfully, you need to stay on top of the news and be creative when it comes to tying an event to your expertise and book. If you can manage that, you can easily elevate your status from an indie author to an expert author.

That is because the need for expert authors is greater on local TV stations. All big TV stations have experts under contract, who get to talk about the important issues of the day. For instance, Dr. Sanjay Gupta is CNN's chief medical correspondent. Even if you wrote an awesome book about a medical topic and can also talk most eloquently about the most complicated medical issues, chances are extremely slim that CNN will put you on air because Dr. Sanjay Gupta is already on their payroll. Local TV does not have that luxury; in other words, this is where you can make yourself a name, and if you go about it with enough tenacity, you probably won't face a lot of competition.

So, how do you go best about finding and preparing a pitch in connection with a current event?

The biggest negative factor is that you have no time to prepare and you have to be quick. On the plus side, the producers, TV anchors, and media personnel are in the same situation. Whereas CNN and the Big Three (ABC, CBS and NBC – national TV) have interns and researchers and basically press a button to get facts and important details, local TV stations do not have the same resources. They rely on expert authors to explain the facts. Naturally, they prefer featuring a local expert author rather than pulling syndicated content. Local TV stations are incredibly community orientated;

they want to show local experts.

To be ready at any time, you have to do some prep work even before you study the news. Start by checking out where the studios of your local TV stations are. For instance, I live in Greenville, SC, where NBC (WYFF) and FOX (WHNS) have local studios.

However, ABC affiliate WLOS's studios are located in Asheville, NC, and CBS affiliate WSPA is located in Spartanburg, SC. Both, Asheville and Spartanburg, are about a fifty minutes drive from where I live.

Most likely, any TV station is going to put you on during the morning news. To be featured in the news at 6:30 a.m., you have to arrive at the studios at 6:00 a.m. I guess you can see why I never pitched WLOS and WSPA. I would have to drive off at 5:00 a.m. in the morning to "make the date" or take a hotel room. Plus, I would have to get up at 3:30 a.m. to look really good at 5:00 a.m. and who on earth looks good at that time of the day?

Once you know which TV studios are close enough for you so can reach them, begin watching these stations' evening news, when syndicated content from their main/national TV station is being aired.

Local affiliates have access to the news clips from their main stations; so, if you can pitch them successfully, the TV station will begin the report with a previously aired TV-clip from the main station. When I had my chance, the news clip began with a picture of Brad Pitt. That's fabulous name association. [It seems to suggest "Brad Pitt and I".]

This event happened in early 2013 when I was still living in Wilmington, NC. In this particular case, only ABC (national) reported the news about Pitt's issues, so the only station I could pitch successfully was ABC affiliate WWAY-3 TV in Wilmington, NC. However, if at the time I would have lived in Greenville, SC, where I live now, my only option would have been to drive one hour to Asheville, NC, where local ABC affiliate WLOS is located.

Of course, it all depends on how much you are willing to do and if your particular situation allows you to pitch TV stations which may be located out of town, but if you focus on the stations in your town, you can be very effective, because they are close.

Your benefit of being featured on TV will be that your name and the title of your book will be listed at the bottom of the TV screen. This leads to face recognition ("I have seen him/her, he/she was on TV") and name recognition. People will begin to see you as an expert. People like to buy books from experts.

If you can't make time at that time of the day, study these TV stations' websites. Make sure that you check out the main sites

http://abcnews.go.com/

http://www.cbsnews.com/

http://www.nbcnews.com/

http://www.foxnews.com/

How Can You Use Your TV-Appearance Most Effectively?

Present pictures of screen prints on your website. Readers of my book *Naked Truths About Getting Book Reviews* know that I recommend to create a newsroom on your website. As suggested in that book, news of your work being featured in newspapers or blogs belongs on this page, but of course, news of a TV appearance belongs there as well. The more newsworthy events you can present on your website, the more likely potential customers will want to buy your book.

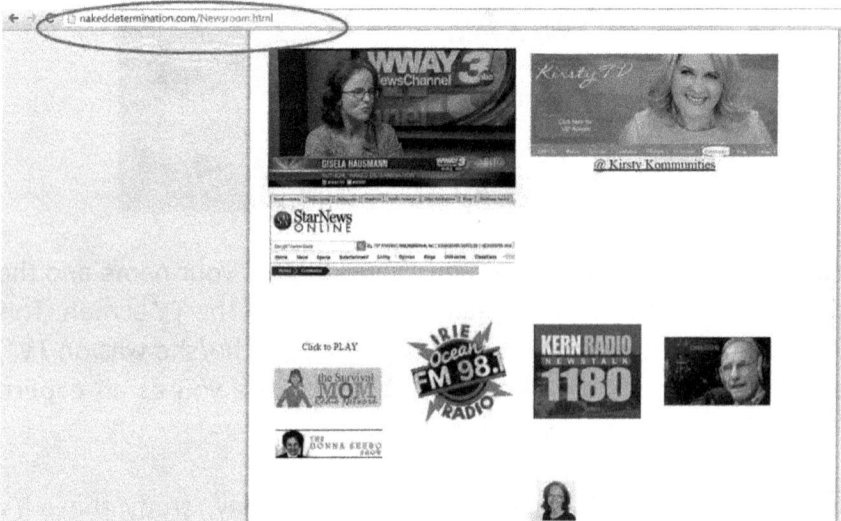

http://nakeddetermination.com/Newsroom.html

Additionally, post a screen print of your appearance(s) on Amazon. If on your Amazon author page you also feature your blog, you have to play around with the order in which you display pictures to show off the items you want potential customers to see first.

Author Updates

Blog post
Why You Should Stop Writing Emails That Sound Like Emails
Jirsak/Shutterstock
Without a doubt, writing best emails is the most effective way to reach influencers. A survey by Good Technology revealed the average...

1 week ago   Read more

Blog post
1 Simple Trick That Leads to More Reviews & SALES!!! (there are 6 more tricks that help even more)
1. It is nothing now that today reviews influence potential buyers' decisions to actually buy, or – not 2. 8 out of 10 shoppers consult online reviews...

3 weeks ago   Read more

Blog post
How to Double up or Triple up on Your Book Promotion
by Gisela Hausmann, author of the "naked, no-fluff marketing books"

Creating a successful book promotion is not easy, but there are ways how...

2 months ago   Read more

blog postings

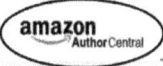

amazon Author Central   **Author Page**   Books   Sales Info ˅   Customer Reviews   Help   Gisela Hausmann ˅

Author Page

Author Pages   Content you provide will appear on Amazon's Gisela Hausmann Page after a short delay.
› Visit Amazon's Gisela Hausmann Page ☐

Biography   edit biography   delete

Her motto:
"Don't wait. The time will never be just right."-Napoleon Hill

Gisela Hausmann is an email evangelist, a PR coach, a communication expert and a life skills artist.

Born to be an adventurer, she also co-piloted single-engine planes, produced movies, and worked in the industries of education, construction, and international transportation. Gisela's friends and fans know her as a woman who goes out to seek the unusual and rare adventure.

A unique mixture of wild risk-taker and careful planner, Gisela globe-trotted almost 100,000 kilometers on three continents, including to the locations of her favorite books: Doctor Zhivago's Russia, Heinrich Harrer's Tibet, and Genghis Khan's Mongolia.

She is also the winner of the
2016 Sparky Award "Best Subject Line"
2016 Honorary Mention Readers Favorite Awards
2016 International Book Awards Finalist
2016 National Indie Excellence Awards Finalist
2015 Kindle Book Awards Finalist
2014 Gold Readers' Favorite... » Read More

Author Page URL   add link   learn more

Create an easy to share link to your Author Page.

Photos   add photo   manage

NOT visible on
Amazon
Author page

[53]

How to Pitch Magazines and News Aggregators

Basically, pitching print publications follows the same principles as pitching TV-stations – you need to offer a story.

Whereas TV-stations will mention your book in the onscreen titles, and hopefully also show the book itself, journalists will mention your book either throughout the text, "xyz, author of (title of book) pointed out..." or add your biography at the end of the article.

Occasionally, I meet authors who worry that a journalist "will steal their ideas..." There is no need to worry. No reputable journalist will steal any ideas; they will also give you full credit because it is in their interest to show that they demonstrated diligence when looking for information and knowledgeable sources.

To pitch magazines and news aggregators correctly, you need to keep in mind the differences between these media outlets.

Newspapers

Unless you can offer a pitch about a topic of local interest, e.g. "Local author reads books at this year's Dr. Seuss Festival. X percent of the proceeds will be donated to our local children's hospital," you probably should not go through the effort to pitch them.

Most local newspapers do not report about books any longer because online publications (including thousands of book blogs) cover this topic extensively. Large newspapers have their own set of rules on how to submit books. Their specific guidelines can be found on the Internet, e.g., here is the link to the New York Times Book Review:

http://www.nytimes.com/content/help/site/books/books.html

Magazines

Magazines are planned and designed months in advance. Three months before a magazine gets on the newsstand, the entire magazine is fully laid out. Also, these days, magazines are being put on shelves two to three weeks before the calendar month actually begins. Most magazines' February issues are on sale by early to mid-January.

This implies you have to plan ahead. If you want to pitch an article related to Valentine's Day (February 14), you need to calculate that the magazine will be out by mid-January. Deduct three months from that date to learn that the February issue is fully planned and laid out by mid-October. To have a chance at pitching the magazine successfully, you need to contact them the latest by mid-September.

Though this sounds difficult, the ROI (return-on-investment) is well worth it. Always remember that an ad in a magazine would cost you thousands of dollars, yet ads have no bragging value; everybody who can afford it can place an ad whereas getting featured in a reputable magazine is something to brag about.

Online Magazines

Many print magazines have online editions that add articles which are not featured in the print editions, every week. Therefore, the time window to pitch them is much shorter – only about two to four weeks. The bragging value is almost as good as being featured in a print magazine.

News Aggregators

A news aggregator is a web application which combines syndicated web content such as online newspapers, blogs, podcasts, and video blogs. The most famous and widely read publication of this kind is the *Huffington Post*. According to the *International Business Times,* in October 2015, the Huffington Post recorded 86 million visitors.

I am a Huffington Post contributor who can tell you that it takes a long time and a portfolio of many interesting blogs to become a contributor. The much faster way to get featured is to pitch a Huffington Post reporter or contributor. Since news aggregators are online publications, you can pitch them anytime.

Two ways to get featured in magazines

a) You become **one of the sources**. An example is featured in this book's chapter "Example of a Successful Pitch to a Magazine Editor."
The easiest way to find such opportunities is to be subscribed to HARO (Help-A-Reporter) https://www.helpareporter.com/.
A second way to become a source is to get invited by a reporter, an anchor, or a host of the news outlet. If they are pleased with your contribution, they will ask you to pitch them if you have newsworthy information and they will also contact you when they have questions.

b) You pitch a media outlet with **your own article**. It is totally up to you to find an angle that will be interesting to the media outlet's readers.

Like all media outlets, most magazines feature a nice mix of traditional articles and totally new material. Certainly, no publication will skip reporting about Christmas or New Year's related topics, at the same time they also look for totally new insights.

Before you pitch any magazine with your own article, read and study at least a dozen of this magazine's articles, ideally, articles that have been shared many times.

1. Copy and paste ten articles in a word document.
2. Perform a word count and calculate the average length of already featured articles; that's how your long your article should be.
3. Study the way the article is written. Some magazines like to begin with a short introduction to the topic; very specialized magazines whose readership consists of people who have advanced knowledge about the magazine's subject matter get straight to the point.
4. Study the biography of the writers. Some magazines feature very short biographies and offer links to the writers' websites. Other magazines offer up to 200 words of biography that describe all of the author's accomplishments. Tailor your biography to the style the magazine prefers.

Ignoring these guidelines will lead to your pitch/article being rejected because there is no faster way to express, "I never read your magazine; I just want you to feature my stuff." Unless you are a celebrity author, this just won't work.

Certainly, pitching magazines is one of the best ways to draw attention to your book(s). Readers who enjoy reading your writings will be interested in reading your books as well.

Additionally, you can tweet-brag about your accomplishments. It's another way of attracting readers/customers and nurturing the funnel. Here is an example of one of my most successful (sales) tweets. This tweet keeps selling books even three years after my book was featured in the magazine.

Naked_Determination @Naked_Determina · 12 Dec 2016
#mondaymotivation
Write best #email #directEmail
#marketingtips #BusinessMgmt
As seen in SUCCESS & in Entrepreneur
smarturl.it/j3zk1c

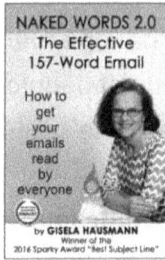

NAKED WORDS 2.0
The Effective
157-Word Email

How to
get
your
emails
read
by
everyone

by GISELA HAUSMANN
Winner of the
2016 Sparky Award "Best Subject Line"

NAKED WORDS 2.0: The Effective 157-Word Email
Kindle Edition
by Gisela Hausmann · (Author), Divya Lavanya (Editor)
★★★★★ · 29 customer reviews

> See all 2 formats and editions

Kindle	Paperback
$4.25	$10.99 √Prime
Read with Our Free App	9 Used from $11.19
	14 New from $9.32

From the winner of the 2016 Sparky Award "Best Subject Line"

"A guide to concise, commanding communiques"
Mary Vinnedge, SUCCESS Magazine

HOW TO GET YOUR EMAILS READ BY EVERYONE

[58]

Example of a Successful Pitch for TV

Here is an example of a real pitch for TV, which I presented to WYFF-4, NBC's affiliate in Greenville, SC.

It is an "unsolicited pitch" which means the person who pitches needs to make their case *why* the anchor, editor, or host should care about this topic, and *why* readers, viewers, and listeners want to know about it.

Notice that I

- suggested a pitch
- researched the perfect time (local graduation ceremonies)
- prepared the background graphics and the bio

~~*~~

Dear (name of anchor),

It's that time of the year! College students are about to graduate.
(graduation ceremony local university #1 (date))
(graduation ceremony local university #2 (date))
(graduation ceremony local university #3 (date))

Are you planning a "Tips for students who looking for their first job or first internship" feature?

The below may be really helpful for our local students:
3 Tips for Email Networking

If you need me to talk about a related subject I can prepare whatever you need.

Of course, I am ready any time.

As always,
Gisela
(xxx) xxx-xxxx

3 Tips for Email Networking

1) Send your email before 6:30 a.m. Chances are your contact will read it within half an hour of you sending it.

- - - (back ground graphics) - - -
- A survey by Good Technology revealed the average American first checks their phone around 7:09 a.m.
- 68 % of people check their work emails before 8 a.m.
- 50 % check their work email while still in bed
- - - (end of back ground graphics) - - -

These numbers prove that email is the best way to reach influencers.

2) What if you are NOT a morning person?

Type your email the day before and save it as a draft. The next day type a blank space at the end of the email, or delete a comma and add it again; in other words, make a tiny change.

(You can do this even if you haven't had your morning coffee!)
Doing this tiny change will set the emails time stamp to this minute; your email will look as you had typed it in the morning.

3) Avoid the word "I" like the plague. Make a conscious effort to replace "I"s with "you"s.

Examples:

DON'T WRITE:
"I want to add you to my network ... "

WRITE:

"You and I have a common interest – (field of interest). Hope you will connect with me ..."

***

DON'T WRITE:

"I saw that you were interested in... "

WRITE:

"You showed an interest in... Can I help with..."

***

DON'T WRITE:

"I would like to introduce myself ..."

WRITE:

"Just briefly: We specialize in... and we can help with... If we can assist you in any way, please send us an e-mail or call xxx-xxx-xxxx."

***

BIO: Gisela Hausmann is the winner of the 2016 Sparky Award "Best Subject line," awarded by SparkPost. Her book *NAKED WORDS 2.0 The Effective 157-Word Email* has been featured in the *SUCCESS* magazine. Her book *NAKED TEXT Email Writing Skills for Teenagers* is a 2016 National Indie Excellence Awards Finalist

~~*~~

(end of pitch)

Basically, this pitch was prepared to a level that the anchor only had to say "yes" or "no"; all "homework" was already done. Indeed, the anchor was happy to invite me.

TIP: Always make sure that you send the text for background graphics in the precise order you want to present them. The anchor will send your text to TV-station's video editor, who will use your text to generate some awesome CGs (computer graphics). They will roll in the order you sent them. Also, video editors do not edit text.

TIP: If you brag *skillfully*, anchors may ask you to present your book live/on air (hold the book during the entire airing of the segment) because TV-anchors are very community-oriented people.

Example of a Successful Pitch to a Magazine Editor

Here is an example of a "solicited pitch." It was a particularly interesting situation. The reporter had posted his query on HARO in the morning; he needed submissions by the end of business day. Unfortunately, because I was out of town, I saw the query only the next day.

Though, on HARO, some reporters post anonymously, this reporter had given his name and also stated that he was looking for submissions for an article in *Publishers Weekly*. Certainly, every author wants to be featured in *Publishers Weekly*, and I too.

Since HARO does not accept submissions which are emailed after the cut-off time, I went on Linkedin to find the journalist. Though there was no guarantee that he would still accept my submission, considering what was at stake, I just had to try.

Query:
    How to Get Self-Published Books into Stores and Libraries

My email:

    Sorry, (name),

    that I missed your deadline @HARO yesterday. I was out of town for an important meeting. Hope you can still use this information.

    1) One of the hurdles for self-published authors who publish their books with Createspace is that Barnes & Noble does not really want to work with Createspace but prefers to work with a distributor like Baker & Taylor.
    2) After I got one of my books featured in a national magazine this barrier fell in seconds. I purchased a copy of

the magazine at B&N and asked to speak to the event manager. Then, I showed her the article and asked if she did not want to invite me. She immediately signed me up for a book signing even though I publish via Createspace.

3) Another thing that helps on a local level is to try to become a to-go person at the local TV-station. I have been a guest at my local station WYFF-4 three times in the last four months.

Backup info (websites)
http://www.giselahausmann.com/newsroom.html
http://stores.barnesandnoble.com/event/9780061722498-0

Thank you, Gisela
(xxx) xxx-xxxx

Bio:
Gisela Hausmann is an email evangelist and communications expert. She publishes her own series of "naked (no-fluff) books." Her book *NAKED WORDS 2.0 The Effective 157-Word Email* was featured in the SUCCESS magazine.
She tweets @Naked_Determina
http://www.giselahausmann.com/

The journalist's reply:

Great! Thanks Gisela--will keep you posted on this feature

The article in Publisher's Weekly:

http://www.publishersweekly.com/pw/by-topic/authors/pw-select/article/68467-how-to-get-self-published-books-into-stores-and-libraries.html

TIP: When you submit a "solicited pitch," meaning that you answer a reporter's very specific question, obviously you do not have to explain why this topic important. Also, if the reporter has a specific topic in mind, stick to the topic; don't venture off to present a completely new angle, and be as brief as possible. Most often you do not know how many contributors the reporter wants to quote. If your reply is too long, and the reporter has to "filter out" or "edit your contribution" your contribution is probably not going to make the cut.

Always provide a bio; bragging is encouraged. Every reporter wants to know that they are quoting an accomplished source.

~ * * * ~

If you need help with this task please check my website giselahausmann.com. I coach authors and small business owners how to get media coverage. My own work has been featured in the *SUCCESS* magazine, in *Entrepreneur,* on *Bloomberg, NBC's Business blog, on Realtor.com, and on FOXNews.* I have also been a guest on TV six times.

~ * * * ~

Free Marketing & PR via Guest Blogging

Building your own blog and attracting a steady following can be difficult; after all, there are already thousands of extremely successful blogs. Therefore, consider guest-blogging.

Some blogs are read by hundreds of thousands of people.

That being said, just like when trying to get on TV, you probably should not start with the cream of the cream but work your way up.

To show you possibilities, here is a list of the world's 50 most powerful blogs:

https://www.theguardian.com/technology/2008/mar/09/blogs

Remember, when you pitch a top-tier blogger, who is NOT a book blogger, you can't pitch your book. You have to pitch a story just as if you would be pitching a TV-host.

Of course, nonfiction authors can always blog about their topic. The author of a cook book could not pitch his book but something thematic, like, for instance

- "7 Soups, perfect for hot summer days"

Equally, a (fiction) author of a romantic novel could not pitch her novel, but something thematic, like, for instance

- "Valentine's Day is coming up, 5 Romantic traditions from the Middle Ages you have never heard about"

A (fiction) Sci-Fi author could pitch

- "Valentine's Day is coming up; 5 Ways how people might date on Mars in the future."

If you wrote a cook book, you can guest blog at any of the hundreds of food blogs, including at foodnetwork.com. In other words, if you don't want to pitch the FOOD NETWORK **TV**, you can always pitch the network's blog, thereby not having to worry if you mess up on TV.

Fiction authors need to be a bit more creative. A writer of trial novels can pitch a legal blog. For instance, the trial of George Zimmerman, who shot Trayvon Martin, was an opportunity to make a connection between this trial and a historic trial about the shooting of an African American man.

Many indie authors make the mistake of blogging too much about author-related tasks.

Instead – Focus on your expertise! Do you write historical novels, maybe love stories that play out in the days when the House of Medici ruled large parts of Italy?

If so, you know a lot about the Medici's power games, banking during the Renaissance, and Renaissance artists whose work we still admire today. Any of these topics will be more interesting to your target group than another blog about "how to use social media platforms to your advantage."

A interesting article about "Bank xyz's latest scandal – Haven't we heard the same scheme happening during the Middle Ages?" could even make it to any of the big business publications.

It's all about creativity! Bloggers love creative people. If any of the major top-tier bloggers would invite you to guest blog for them, your work would get exposed to many people you would not meet any other way.

Sometimes, the one or other blogger will even come to you, directly, because they have noticed your work, most often a guest blog. Therefore, most certainly, guest blogging needs to be understood as a huge opportunity.

However, as in every industry, there are some people who make you work harder than they do. Here is how to identify them:

1. Regardless of whether you find an inquiry on HARO or whether a blogger approaches you directly – check them out.

2. Search for both, "blogger AND blog" on Google. (It is important that you search for both because some bloggers and journalists blog for various sites. To find out the complete scope, you need precise data.)

3. Once you have found the specific blog where you want to guest blog or others who want you to guest blog for them, click the link to the blogger's Twitter account.

4. Check how many tweeps follow the blog *and* the blogger, how often blogs get re-tweeted, and most importantly if the main blogger gives guest bloggers a shout-out.

5. Giving a shout-out on Twitter is easy; it is also common courtesy.

6. If the main blogger does not give guest bloggers at least one (1) shout-out, he might be letting the guest bloggers work for him – for free.

Here is what a proper shout-out looks like
"Title of blog" http://www.xyz-blog.com/xyz-blog/how-to/blog/2016/06/6-blog_title.html ... **via @(guestblogger)** @xyz-blog

Guest blogging is supposed to be a mutual thing.

"You blog for me... I give you exposure to my crowd... you re-tweet to give me exposure to your crowd..." – It is a type of digital network sharing.

There are some bloggers who will put your work on their website but will not give you a shout-out. You can spot them easily when checking their Twitter feed.

TIP: Check if the main blogger gives *any* other blogger a shout-out by tweeting a **"via @(name_of_guestblogger)"**-annotation.
If they don't, chances are they won't do it for you.

Of course, if you decide to guest blog for a blogger who won't give shout-outs, that does not hinder you to tweet your own blog to your own followers. However, it means that the main blogger isn't "advertising" on Twitter that you are an influencer.

If you face such a scenario, you need to decide if you want to guest blog for this website. It may or may not be a good idea.

Always weigh all of your options. Robert DeNiro did not start out playing Vito Corleone in "The Godfather II." His first role was a small uncredited part in a foreign (French) movie, "Three Rooms in Manhattan" directed by Marcel Carné.

All of us have to start little. Maybe being featured on a reputable site is a good deal even if you don't get a shout-out, because you can still feature this accomplishment on your website to build your own reputation, just like in 1965 Robert DeNiro's resume included only one foreign movie.

There is also another group of bloggers who won't give you a shout-out; they are mostly nonfiction industry bloggers. Probably, sooner or later, this type of blogging will also be taken over by book bloggers.

This type of bloggers do not blog a real blog of 700 to 2,100 words but blog mini-blog collections. Typically, once per month, they invite their circle of bloggers to answer a question, like, for instance, "Your Best Way to Improve a Marketing Email" or "Who is the Business Person who impresses you the Most?"

Upon receiving the invited contributors' mini-blogs of less than 150 words, the blogger combines them into one long blog, for instance "(x number of) Best Ways to Improve a Marketing Email."

All contributors receive credit with a link to their website of choice (which could be their website, their own blog, or a social media profile) next to their contribution.

Once the blog is published, the contributors get informed. It is the contributors' "duty" to share the blog on social media platforms, at least once and up to "as often as you like."

If you get invited to become a contributor to this type of blog, I would advise you to participate for various reasons:

- Since many "mini-bloggers/influencers" share the same blog, other influencers are spreading the word too; you'll benefit from their actions. This type of blog is a truly interesting form of digital network sharing.
- Writing a mini-blog of about 150 words is not too much work.
- It's fun and challenging to find answers to the many different questions.
- If you also read the blog and study other contributors' mini-blogs, you'll find out who other movers and shakers in your industry/in your genre are.

On the plus side, it is a lot of fun to be a part of such a circle; on the minus side, this type of blog usually doesn't have too much depth but represents a collection of thoughts.

I am a member of two such bloggers' circles where I have met quite a few very interesting people. It's fun, it's fast, and it's interesting! 5 stars! Highly recommended.

Example:

53. "The Next Great Idea"

"The next great idea" to sell more goods/services is asking for lots of reviews. Studies prove that 8/10 people consult reviews when making the decision to buy. There are 6 different kinds of reviews ("Love this", typical, technical, venting, funny, & short story). All appeal to different buyers.

Reviews are "gifts that keep on giving". They can be "reused" for years to come, in fliers, in social media posts, and in radio and TV ads, by writing or saying "see our x number of reviews on..."

Thanks to: Gisela Hausmann of Gisela Hausmann.

← Link to website

Monitor Your Book's Media Coverage

If you get into the habit of pitching traditional media outlets as well as bloggers regularly, you'll notice that sometimes it can take a long time until the blogs in which your work is featured actually go "live."

Most often the blogger will notify you, but sometimes they won't.

Additionally, sometimes blogs get "picked up and reblogged" on another site. For instance, when Realtor.com featured a few of my tips about how to build an outdoor fireplace, FOXNews picked up that same blog and presented it on its website, which lead to additional Facebook sharing and retweeting of the same content.

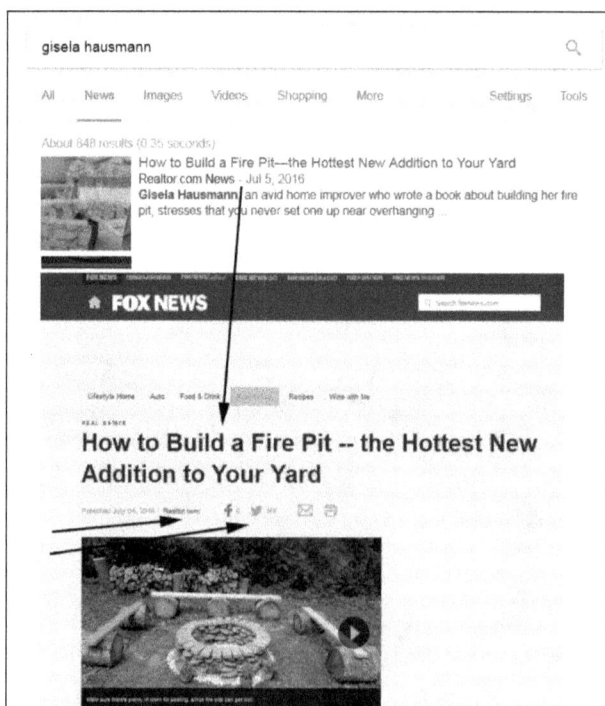

Since you can't know which news organizations might want to re-blog "your" content always apply your best effort; it may help you to get "your content" re-blogged on many sites and to many different audiences. Yahoo and the Huffington Post are the best known news aggregators.

TIP: Use blogging and guest-blogging to help build your funnel and monitor the results.

When you do, be sure to click "news" before you click the search button, otherwise you'll get to see only your own website and your books' listings on Amazon.

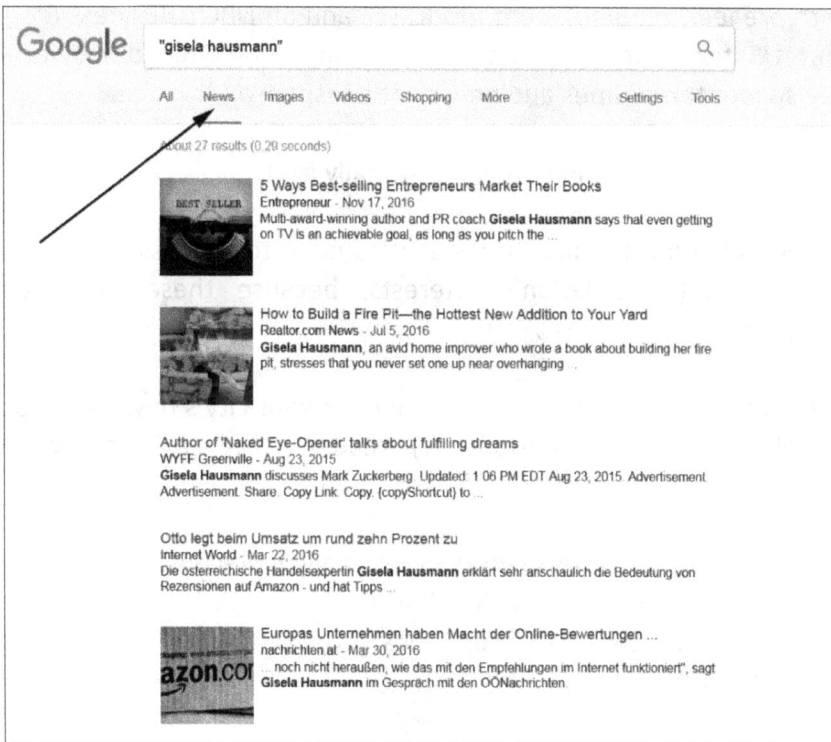

TIP: If your work gets featured on a TV-station's blog, always pull a screen print of the complete article. In contrast to online newspapers, TV-stations delete older blogs periodically. If you did not pull a screen-print, you may lose the proof that you were featured at an important news outlet.

A Surprising Revelation About Media Coverage

Maybe you have already tried pitching your local newspaper, local magazines, and similar publications, but you just could not get their attention.

So, here comes my surprise revelation: Maybe you didn't succeed because you didn't shoot for the stars!

My books have been featured in the *SUCCESS* magazine, in *Entrepreneur*, on *Bloomberg* (podcast), and on NBC's Business Blog, four US top notch publications; in contrast, I pitched my local newspaper three times and never got a response.

Though this may sound ridiculous, it really isn't.

In general, a local publication's articles need to address a majority of the local population's interests, because these are their customers.

TIP: You can look up the demographics of your city's newspaper by googling "(name of newspaper) reader stats" or "(name of newspaper) media kit."

In contrast to local newspapers, most really well-known magazines focus on specific themes, like business, or music, or women's interests; very often these magazines' journalists focus on a specific topic within the larger theme.

This makes it a bit easier to pitch magazine editors; you only need to google your specific topic to see who wrote about it in the past, and therefore may want to write about a similar topic, again.

The best part about pitching an expert journalist is that you don't have to explain **why** "your topic" is important. They know because they write about your specific topic. For instance, if you write love stories, you can pitch your local newspaper all day long and probably won't get a response because your local paper would only present news about the publication of a love story from a celebrity author.

In contrast, every issue of *Woman's World* features a love story in the back of the magazine. *Woman's World* has a circulation of 1.6 million readers and you can pitch them.

Equally, even though pretty much everybody uses email to communicate with business partners, I would have a harder time, "selling" a local journalist why they should feature an article about "writing best emails" when they could fill that same space with an article about a local harvest festival, which 500 people from my community attended. The simple truth is that 500 people in my community may buy the paper only to see what the newspaper wrote about the harvest fair, but the same people aren't looking for an article about "writing best emails."

TIP: If you want to be featured in your local paper try to do a book signing at a local charity event or local festival, which will be covered by your local paper.

Most likely you read a specific magazine regularly, because it features topics that interest you and which you also write about. For instance, there are at least half a dozen of awesome magazines about poetry.

You know these publication's style, what they feature and what's important to their editors and audiences, just like I knew what's important to the readers of the *SUCCESS* magazine. Since I read this magazine every month, I had an easier time pitching my book to them.

TIP: Don't be shy but pitch your favorite magazine!

Free Marketing & PR via Twitter Promotions

Twitter's 2016 statistics reveal some good news for authors. Though only about a third of the number of people who use Facebook (68% of all U.S. adults) use Twitter (21% of all U.S. adults), Twitter is popular among highly educated people. 29% of internet users with college degrees use Twitter. It is probably fair to assume that highly educated people like to read.

Additionally, in 2016, Twitter continued to improve its features.

- Twitter users can now retweet their own tweets,

- Twitter's new limit for videos got increased to 140 seconds (two minutes and 20 seconds)

- Media attachments (e.g. images) and quoted tweets are no longer counted toward the 140 character limit; therefore, tweets containing these items can now be longer.

Twitter is also testing a variety of new features. To stay up-to-date, please follow Twitter's blog https://blog.Twitter.com.

Personally, I have been a huge fan of genius internet entrepreneur Jack Dorsey since I noticed his work as the co-founder and CEO of Twitter, in 2009. That's why I tried to search for specific ways indie authors can promote their books on Twitter already two years ago. The result of my research was that writing a book about this topic may not be the best idea. A nonfiction book's knowledge should stay relevant at least for one year, but on Twitter things can change very quickly.

Still, a few months ago, I noticed a fact that could be true for most indie authors for a prolonged time period: Twitter users like to share tweets about books that can be borrowed from public libraries.

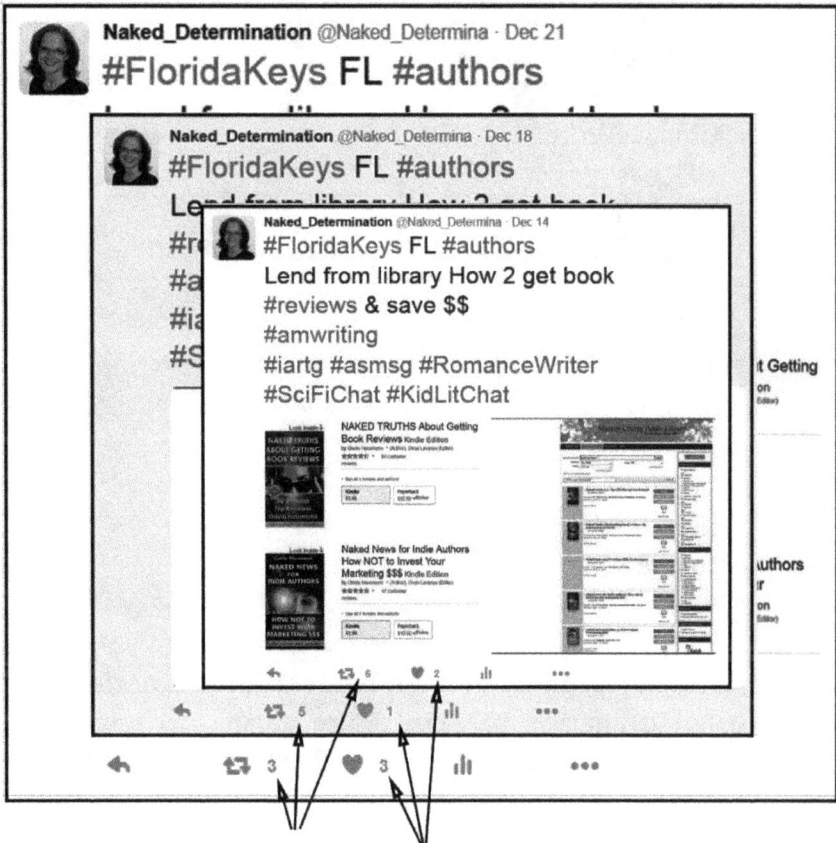

It is also a concept that can be used to "nurture the funnel."

1. Most everybody likes public libraries.
2. A tweet that a book can be found in a specific library is never a sales pitch.
3. Anybody who re-tweets such a tweet demonstrates that they are trying to help their followers who may be living in the area where the library is located.
4. By using the city's hashtag, indie authors can attract new followers from the cities where the libraries are located who might otherwise never find them.

5. Tweeting news about books in libraries with the added author hashtags
#AmWriting
#WriterWednesday
#WritersLife
#IndieAuthors
#RomanceWriter
#SciFiChat
#KidLitChat
#MemoirChat
#FlashFic
#Romance
#Horror
#FanFic
#YA
#History
#FridayReads
#MustRead
#StoryFriday

also attracts new followers because Twitter users like useful tweets that are not connected to sales. More about this topic in my chapter about getting books in public libraries.

Of course, I also looked into the topic of paid Twitter promotions. The simplicity of Twitter's structure suggests that tweeting is a marketing task which can be "outsourced" much easier than other activities.

To increase the success rate of Twitter promotions, indie authors can explore these three elements before buying:

1) the Twitter account itself

Of the three item on this list this one can be done fastest. To check for fake followers go to:

https://www.twitteraudit.com/

https://www.socialbakers.com/

https://fakers.statuspeople.com/

The three organizations back up their services with different methods; therefore it may pay off to run all three reports.

It is important to know that the presence of fake followers does not mean that the account holder purchased followers. The fake Twitter accounts could also be spam bots generated by automated software. Still, fake Twitter accounts do not purchase books.

2) the Followers' profiles

Though more labor intensive, this is a fun task which you should probably handle on a desktop. That will allow you to see more profiles at one glance.

Instead of checking out the Twitter account's tweets, study its followers' profiles. Many, if not most, avid readers list their interests in their Twitter profiles. You might even discover people who you want to follow.

Then again, if you want to promote your specific genre book, and you can't spot a significant number of followers whose profile suggests an interest in your topic, you might want to reevaluate your plan.

Unfortunately, these two elements do not provide a complete picture.

These days, it is customary for book marketing services providers to attract followers by running a Kindle Fire Give-away. Which implies that many Twitter account holders who offer this incentive may gain legitimate followers, who read books. However, it's possible these followers may not read more than half-a-dozen books per year. They may have joined for a chance to win a Kindle Fire.

Therefore, the only way to get even better data is to check.

3) the Ads

Be warned! This can be a laborious task.

As an author, you know your book's genre best. By checking the rankings of books, which are already being advertised, maybe even following some books for one week, you will be able to judge successful campaigns and evaluate the elements that make successful campaigns successful.

TIP: The best way to do this is to create a spreadsheet on which you record the sales ranking of books that are currently advertised for a few days, or as long as they are being promoted. Though you won't know sales numbers you can see how the book's sales rank improves, or not.

Then, evaluate specific details. Books from certain genres get better results with picture ads (romance), others attract buyers with mysterious questions (thriller, horror), and again others do well presenting quotes from reviews (nonfiction).

Of course, none of these methods will accurately forecast how many books you might sell with a Twitter promotion, but doing this research may help you plan a best campaign.

Paid Book Reviews

There are quite many paid book review services who advertise that their reviews help improve the credibility of books and generate sales.

Please make no mistake: ALL authentic, emotional, well-written reviews help generate sales. In fact, real reader reviews have the additional side benefit that readers who review your book will also tell their friends about your book.

In contrast, when have you heard somebody say "I read about this book on a paid review service's website"?

Also, many readers share reviews on social media websites but I have yet to see a paid book review service's tweet that got retweeted more than a dozen times.

As the author of *NAKED TRUTHS About Getting Book Reviews,* I do not believe that buying one or more book reviews should be a first choice for indie authors. However, having interviewed quite a few librarians, I know that they put a lot of value on certain paid book reviews, most notably Kirkus' book reviews. In fact, librarians study Kirkus' magazine religiously. However, they do not buy all recommended books but only books that fit in their collections.

If you aim to sell your book(s) to public libraries, college libraries, government organizations, you may have to entertain the thought of purchasing a review.

Considering that I am a review expert, it may come as a surprise that indeed I ordered two reviews from Kirkus.

These are my two stories. Please note that these are anecdotal stories. In no way do I mean to implicate that this could happen to you, but it is what happened to me.

I ordered my first book review from Kirkus in November 2013. I submitted my book *NAKED DETERMINATION: 41 Stories About Overcoming Fear* which had won Bronze at the eLit awards the same year. The following year it would go on to win Gold at the Readers Favorite Awards, 2014.

Because I was in a hurry pursuing a specific plan I even ordered Kirkus' Express Service (4-6 weeks) which costs US$ 575.00.
($425 + $150)

To sum up the experience – for me, the author, it had a surprising outcome; but not in a good way, because I know my book's content. Though trying to stay objective, I noted various "issues" with the review Kirkus provided.

https://www.kirkusreviews.com/book-reviews/gisela-hausmann/naked-determination/

In the opening sentence the reviewer notes that I was born in Austria. A few sentences later, the same reviewer writes,

> "... she traveled **through** Austria and Moscow by bus when she was in her teens... " – *Kirkus Reviews*

"I traveled through Austria"? [... *Hello?! – I used to live in Austria. This fact is mentioned in my book 23 times. How is one supposed to get around without "traveling through one's home country"?*]

Even more perplexing is the wording

> "... she traveled through **Austria** and **Moscow** by bus when she was in her teens and across the **Trans-Siberian Railway** in her 20s..." – *Kirkus Reviews*

Surely anybody who has ever looked at a world map will find this sentence *extremely* awkward.

The reviewer uses parallelism to group similar items, in this case geographical locations. However, "the items" aren't similar at all.

- Austria is a country.

- Moscow is a city, about 1,200 miles east-north-east of Austria.

- The Trans-Siberian Railway is the longest railway line in the world. (5,772 miles).

Consequently, though grammatically correct, this sentence construction *sounds* as if the reviewer is trying something similar to cramming the story of *"Around the World in 80 Days"* in one sentence.

But, that's *not* what the reviewer did.

Readers who read this review and choose to read my book will be extremely surprised to find out that my book also contains travel stories from England, China, Mongolia, Tibet, and the secluded Kashmir region in India, all of which I *also traveled in my 20s*.

That makes the list of travel destinations the reviewer picked incomplete. It also makes it obvious that the reviewer decided to pick travel locations based on "personal preference."

One must wonder what caused the reviewer to mention that I traveled through my home country but to never mention that I traveled to Lhasa, Tibet where I got to meditate in His Holiness the 14th Dalai Lama's former bedroom, for thirty minutes, alone by myself, in 1988.

Since then, hundreds of people have told me how they envy me for experiencing this once-in-a-lifetime opportunity. Most certainly, my story describing these events has to carry more weight than the fact that I traveled through my home country.

This Kirkus review cheats people who might be interested to read first-hand accounts of traveling to the spiritual leader and Nobel Peace Prize Laureate's home country out of finding out that my book contains such a story.

Then again, maybe the reviewer did not select travel locations based on personal preference; maybe, the reviewer never read the complete book but merely skimmed through.

Lastly, the reviewer classified my book *NAKED DETERMINATION: 41 Stories About Overcoming Fear* as a memoir though it is really a life-skills book. It also won two awards in the genre "motivational/ inspirational," not in the genre "biographies and memoirs."

If my evaluation of Kirkus' review sounds like nit-picking to you, consider that this review cost $425.

At around five to six hours of reading time that's about $77 per hour. One would think at this hourly rate, the reviewer would ponder which one of my travel stories they should mention in order to provide best value for Kirkus' review readers.

Unfortunately, these issues weren't the only problems.

As mentioned, I had ordered the Express Service, which costs an additional $150.

Here is the timeline of events:

KIRKUS INDIE
Get Reviewed. Get Discovered.

Kirkus Reviews Home | Kirkus' Book Editing Services | Look Up My

Questions? Contact us: 888-285-Y394 or Indie@kirkus

How It Works | About Our Reviews | Blogs | FAQs | Purchase

YOUR AUTHOR DASHBOARD
NAKED DETERMINATION

Return to this page anytime using the "Look Up My Order" tool above, and the order ID:

Review Status

Place order

Submit book
received Nov. 21, 2013

Download review
view file
returned Dec. 30, 2013

Publish review
learn more
published Jan. 14, 2014

○ Promote review
learn more

Files

Manuscript
view file

Cover
view file

UPLOAD NEW COVER
(JPG, TIF, PNG)
Select file

Browse...

No file selected.

Upload

* Kindly note that because we begin the review process immediately after receiving a submission, we review the original manuscript submitted and cannot permit substitutions. You may, however, update your cover image any time.

DECEMBER 2013

SUNDAY	MONDAY	TUESDAY	WEDNESDAY	THURSDAY	FRIDAY	SATURDAY
1	2	3	4	5	6	7
8	9	10	11	12	13	14
15	16	17	18	19	20	21
22	23	24	25	26	27	28
29	30	31				

(O) 0 on the 20th, 1 on the 27th

2, 3, 4, 5

Delivery (w/ incorrect price) on the 30th

December Holidays
Christmas - 25
New Year's Eve - 31

JANUARY 2014

SUNDAY	MONDAY	TUESDAY	WEDNESDAY	THURSDAY	FRIDAY	SATURDAY
			1	(6)	3	4
5	6	7	8	9	10	11
12	13	(X) 14	15	16	17	18
19	20	21	22	Review finally online 24		25

November Holidays
Daylight Savings Ends
Veterans Day - 11
Thanksgiving - 28

| 17 | 18 | 19 | 20 | 21 | 22 | 23 |
| 24 | 25 | 26 | 27 | 28 | 29 | 30 |

1) Kirkus should have delivered the latest by Friday, January 3, 2014, but they delivered two work days early, on December 30.

2) When they sent me the review I noticed an error. At the time, I had a Christmas-to-New-Year-Sale going on, which prompted Kirkus to list this sale price. Right away, I notified Kirkus via email.

Dear Kirkus Indie Customer Program,

I have received your review as attached.
Please correct the following before publishing:

The price of my ebook Naked Determination is really $ 3.95. It was/is on holiday promotion from Christmas till December 31, 2013.
On January 2, 2014 Naked Determination's ebook edition will be reset to that price.
Please do correct that before you publish the review.
After correcting this detail, the permission to publish is given.

With many thanks,
Gisela Hausmann

---

pls note IMPORTANT: price correction & approval   People

Gisela Hausmann <gisela.hausmann@yahoo.com>   12/30/13 at 9:30 PM
To indiecustomer@kirkus.com, Gisela Hausmann

Dear Kirkus Indie Customer Program,

I have received your review as attached.
Please correct the following before publishing:

The price of my ebook *Naked Determination* is really $ 3.95. It was/is on holiday promotion from Christmas till December 31, 2013.
On January 2, 2014 *Naked Determination*'s ebook edition will be reset to that price.
Please do correct that before you publish the review.

After correcting this detail, the permission to publish is given.

With many thanks,

Gisela Hausmann

The email went unanswered for an entire week.

On January 7, I sent a second email and received the following reply on January 8:

> *Hi Gisela,*
>
> *I apologize. Due to the holidays and the terrible weather we have been in and out of the office.*
>
> *I will make the correction.*
>
> *Thank you for your patience and understanding.*
> *All best,*
> *(name/signature)*

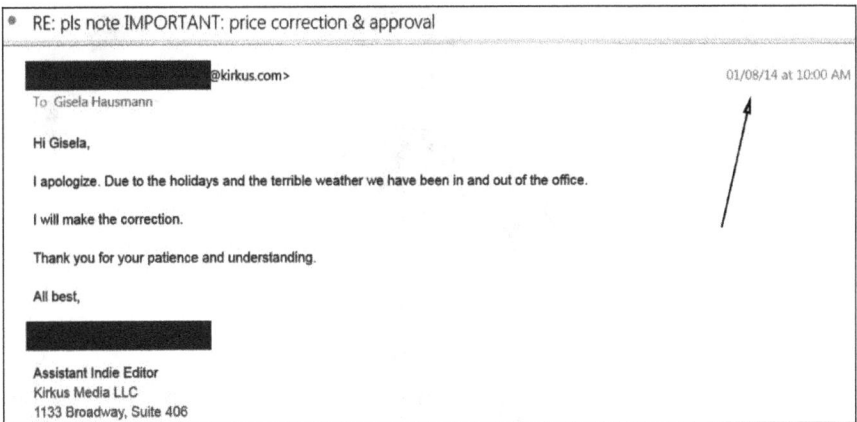

RE: pls note IMPORTANT: price correction & approval

◼︎▬▬▬▬▬▬▬▬▬▬@kirkus.com>   01/08/14 at 10:00 AM

To Gisela Hausmann

Hi Gisela,

I apologize. Due to the holidays and the terrible weather we have been in and out of the office.

I will make the correction.

Thank you for your patience and understanding.

All best,

▬▬▬▬▬▬▬▬▬▬

Assistant Indie Editor
Kirkus Media LLC
1133 Broadway, Suite 406

However, *again*, the review was not posted online, even though I had paid $150 for Express Service.

Finally, on January 14, 2014 I requested that Kirkus returns the handling fee for the Express Delivery.

Here is their reply:

⊛ RE: pls note IMPORTANT: price correction & approval

To Gisela Hausmann

@kirkus.com>

Hi Gisela,

Thanks so much for your message.

Your review was returned to you via the author dashboard before the Express deadline. That is what we guarantee as per our Customer Agreement (https://www.kirkusreviews.com/legal/indie-customer-agreement/). In addition, per our Customer Agreement, we do not provide refunds of any kind.

Thanks so much and once again I do apologize for the delay in publication and appreciate your understanding.

All best,

Assistant Indie Editor
Kirkus Media LLC
1133 Broadway, Suite 406
New York , **NY** 10010

[88]

Hi Gisela,

Thanks so much for your message.

Your review was returned to you via the author dashboard before the Express deadline. That is what we guarantee as per our Customer Agreement (https://www.kirkusreviews.com/legal/indie-customer-agreement/). **In addition, per our Customer Agreement, we do not provide refunds of any kind.**

Thanks so much and once again I do apologize for the delay in publication and appreciate your understanding.

All best,

(name)

Considering that Kirkus prides itself with excellent quality standards, for me this event was a negative experience on many levels. The last reply was also a bit baffling because Kirkus must know that indie authors share their experiences.

Still, in 2016, I did it again. In the meantime I was working on getting my books in public libraries and I wanted to test if indeed a book review from Kirkus really helps to speed up the process. Having published ten books since 2013, I selected my book *NAKED TEXT Email Writing Skills for Teenagers.*

The book is a two-time award winner but I chose it for a different reason. *NAKED TEXT Email Writing Skills for Teenagers* is a niche book; it's literally one of a kind.

To see proof, please see Amazon's selection about this topic:

NAKED TEXT Email Writing Skills for Teenagers Oct 9, 2015
by Gisela Hausmann and Divya Lavanya

Paperback
$12⁹⁹ ✓Prime
Get it by **Saturday, Nov 26**

More Buying Choices
$8.96 used & new (20 offers)

Kindle Edition
$3⁸⁹

It's Not Always Easy (High School Writing Project 2.0 #3) Nov 20, 2013
by Danica Myerson and Stephanie Duncan

Kindle Edition
$0.00 kindleunlimited
Subscribers read for free.

$0⁹⁹ to buy

Dear My Blank: Secret Letters Never Sent Nov 1, 2016
by Emily Trunko and Lisa Congdon

Hardcover
$11²⁴ $14.99 ✓Prime
Get it by **Saturday, Nov 26**

More Buying Choices
$7.16 used & new (43 offers)

Kindle Edition
$9⁹⁹

NAKED TEXT Email Writing Skills for Teenagers by Gisela Hausmann (2
by Gisela Hausmann

Paperback
$66.36 used & new (4 offers)

Sketching and Drawing Pencils Professional Art Set 33 Pieces Essential
by NiL-Tech

$34⁹⁹ $38.95 ✓Prime

Also, the fact that at the time Kirkus offered a special sale helped me in making the decision; Kirkus' reduced price was $350.

Considering my previous experiences, I wanted to make sure that Kirkus was aware that my book is a niche book. And so I added this important tidbit to the information sheet Kirkus wanted me to provide with my book.

Undeniably, today writing/reviewing a niche book is a rare thing.

Here is the review Kirkus' reviewer penned:

https://www.kirkusreviews.com/book-reviews/gisela-hausmann/naked-text-email-writing-skills-teenagers/

This time Kirkus awarded my book with a favorable review. Their "verdict sentence" was:

> "Snappy, useful chat about email importance and etiquette." – *Kirkus Reviews*

There was no mentioning of the fact that my book is a niche-book, though this information could be especially helpful to librarians*.

> [*Many US libraries offer programs to teach people including children and senior citizens digital skills. According to Pew Research 47% of Americans agree libraries contribute "a lot" to providing a trusted place for people to learn about new technologies.
> http://www.pewinternet.org/2016/09/09/libraries-2016/]

Instead, the reviewer noted,

"Hausmann (*Naked News for Indie Authors How Not to invest Your Marketing $$$*, 2016, etc.) proclaims her primer is "a non-fluff, no-nonsense book." **For the most part**, she is right: her email protocols provide common-sense suggestions for emoji-obsessed teens, especially the excellent tip that readers link to their professional websites or portfolios in email signatures. She does **include some fluff,** however, listing websites of teenaged entrepreneurs, which **seems like filler in this slim book**." – *Kirkus Reviews*

Here is a depiction of "the filler":

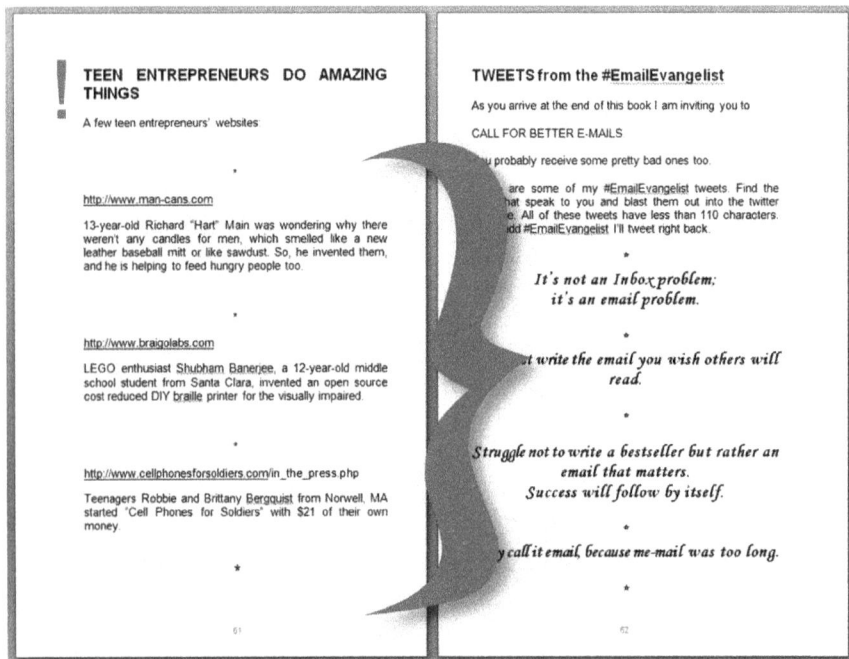

It is one (1) page!

Can one page be called a filler? I'll leave this to your judgment and invite you to think if your book might have similar "*issues.*"

Of course, there is a reason why I added this page. (I used to teach high school and have created hundreds of lesson plans.) This book is written for students. Every teacher will confirm that to teach effectively, teachers have to show the students possible applications of what to do with the new knowledge. If students aren't getting inspired to apply the new knowledge, they forget what they learned.

It seems to me that every educated person who attended high school and college should know that, simply because they must have been exposed to this teaching style for one-and-a-half decades. Already suspicious about Kirkus' reviewers' level of involvement when reading books, I had even added this information on my submission sheet:

> *"... Lastly, the book suggests ideas how young people can use their newly learned skills to make a difference in others' lives..."*

Apparently, it did not help the reviewer understand why this "one page filler" was presented in my book.

*

What is to be learned from my two anecdotal stories about buying two reviews from Kirkus?

Even if your book contains unusual/remarkable content (like my story about getting to meditate in the Dalai Lama's bedroom) there is no guarantee that it will be mentioned in the review.

Even if a nonfiction book presents content according to established industry practices (like my offering applications students might be very interested to learn about), there is a possibility the reviewer may not see it this way.

However, these two stories are purely anecdotal. If you submit your book, Kirkus may very well come to the conclusion that your work is riveting and that you deserve to be called the "next Hemingway."

One fact needs to be pointed out though: If you decide to get a review for the same purpose as I did when I submitted my second book, namely to bring your book to the attention of librarians, consider Kirkus' numbers:

On their website Kirkus states that they present forty (40) book reviews in each issue of their magazine, which they publish twice a month. Kirkus' editors choose these forty reviews. As stated in their fine print section, purchasing a review does not guarantee that the book review will be published in Kirkus' magazine or online newsletter.

On their website https://www.kirkusreviews.com/prize/faq/
Kirkus states that they review between 8,000 and 10,000 books per year.

2 issues x 12 months x 40 reviews = 960 reviews which get published in Kirkus' magazine that gets sent to libraries and industry influencers.

That gives you a 1:8 to 1:10 chance that your book review will be presented to librarians.

It seems I got lucky. Kirkus' review of my *NAKED TEXT Email Writing Skills for Teenagers* got featured in Kirkus' December 01, 2016: Volume LXXXIV, No 23 magazine.

If a book review is favorable but *not* featured in Kirkus' magazine or newsletter, its author will need to do the marketing to libraries themselves, and also pay for it, themselves.

Authors can call libraries' acquisition departments, email them, send them some form of mailing, or even visit local libraries in person.

To find the public libraries of US states you can research webpages following this system:

http://www.publiclibraries.com/**alabama**.htm
http://www.publiclibraries.com/**alaska**.htm
http://www.publiclibraries.com/**arizona**.htm

As a second step, you need to copy and paste the libraries' names into your web browser to find the libraries' actual webpages that contain their contact information.

TIP: If you go this route and check out web pages of public libraries, always see if they also host a book club. Many library web pages mention regular library activities. Make a note of such findings, so you can approach the book club in the event that this library decides to add your book to their collection. I would assume that most members of book clubs are also on Goodreads, where they probably post reviews. That could lead to exponentially bigger exposure.

It is important to know that libraries are not spontaneous buyers but organizations that spend their budget according to their organization's guidelines.

Once Kirkus' magazine arrives at a library, it gets circulated to the various reference librarians. They check off the books they feel they need to add to their collections. Then, the magazine gets passed to the library's acquisition department, which buys the selected books according to their budgeting guidelines and timely relevance.

If, for instance, you published a book with Christmas stories, which is featured in one of Kirkus' two November magazines, a reference librarian may mark your book as a desired purchase. However, the acquisitions department may not be able to allocate the funds for this purchase immediately. Since the book is a seasonal book, the library may acquire this book only in the following fall.

Obviously, this is an extreme example because Christmas happens only once per year but it illustrates how this system works.

Summing it up, if you can make a case for your book, you may not need to purchase a review; maybe you feel that saving $425 and investing only a fraction of this amount in contacting libraries directly is a better choice. Still, all authors need to **impress** librarians (even famous authors).

*

Other notable paid review services:

IndieReader
http://indiereader.com/authorservices/indie-book-reviews/

Self-Publishing Review
http://www.selfpublishingreview.com/get-reviewed/

BlueInk Review
https://www.blueinkreview.com/purchase/

Learn to Plan Getting Your Book Into Public Libraries, Strategically

A library's shelf space is valuable, just like shelf space in a book store. Libraries add only books their patrons want or need to read.

Consequently, to get a public library or a college library to "add your book," meaning they buy it or you donate it, you have to make a case that potential readers will be looking for your book.

Certainly, you can make this case easiest in your hometown. Every librarian understands that you have friends who want to read your book but may not want to purchase it. Lots of people do that, for various reasons, which is why public libraries exist.

Beyond your hometown, there may be libraries in other cities, who may be interested in adding your book. Though I live in Greenville, SC now, I used to live in Key Largo, FL for sixteen years. I also taught high school there. You can probably imagine that my former colleagues and students could be very interested in reading my book *NAKED DETERMINATION: 41 Stories About Overcoming Fear,* especially my former students. Indeed, the Key Largo library purchased my book in 2014 on the occasion of my book winning Gold at the Readers Favorite Awards.

TIP: Book awards help to make your case.

Making your case to librarians in cities you have never even visited can be a bit more complicated. You need to plan this endeavor strategically.

First, you should check if your book isn't already in libraries. (I noticed that even the book of a European author friend found its way into US public libraries.)

Go to Worldcat.org and see if your book can be found in any library. Unfortunately, WorldCat is not all inclusive but it may help you in finding out things you don't know.

As its name suggests, WorldCat lists data from libraries worldwide. In the provided example, you can see that my book *obvious LETTERS* (published in 1998) found its way in the United States Army's European Region Library in Heidelberg, 4400 miles from where I live. And, another copy is located in the National Library Board in Singapore, 9900 miles from where I live.

Of course, these two sales did not make me rich but I still get a kick out of knowing which library's collections feature my books. Also, the fact that overseas libraries bought my book might have impressed librarians who considered buying my book.

WorldCat also informs that my book *obvious LETTERS* can be found in US libraries in Fort Wayne, IN, Centereach, NY, Guthrie, TX, Kemmerer, WY, Lewistown, MT and Wenatchee, WA.

To be honest, though in 1998 I sold this book via Amazon, I did not know about WorldCat then, if it even was available on the Internet. Thus I cannot tell you whether the overseas libraries purchased the book first or the American libraries.

Some US states (GA, IN, MA, MO, NC, OR, SD, WA) use their own library systems instead of registering books with WorldCat. (This information is listed in the addendum of this book.)

Regardless, whether your book has already been added to libraries or not, a strategic plan can help in getting your book into more libraries.

While I cannot be sure that the following suggestions are true for *all* US libraries, I have heard the following generalizations from librarians:

Potentially <u>very</u> interesting genres:

- Nonfiction

- Love stories (many people love to read this genre but don't want to buy every book they read)
- Sci-Fi
- Historical novels
- Children's books
- YA

Less interesting genres:

- Memoirs (unless you are celebrity)
- Erotica (many readers read erotica on e-readers exclusively)
- Life Skills/Self-Help (too much competition from celebrity authors)

Contacting libraries and marketing your book(s) to them can be labor intensive if you decide to call or email them. Sending libraries postcards or fliers doesn't have to be too expensive if you design your mailing cleverly

- postage for postcards is cheaper than for letters
- flyers can be folded and may not need an envelope
- printing in black and white print is cheaper than printing in color

US Postal Service™ rates:

> **Letter** Stamps
> Standard-sized, rectangular envelopes From **$0.47**
> Square, Oversized, or Unusual Envelopes From **$0.68**
>
> **Postcard** Stamps
> Standard-sized, rectangular envelopes From **$0.34**

As always, the easiest and cheapest option might be to visit your local library in person.

If you published more than one book, it pays off to decide which one(s) you should market.

As the author of books from various nonfiction genres, my first step was to put together a chart to help me figure out which ones of my books I should market.

I finally decided to market only four of my books to libraries because I did not want to look obnoxious by trying to talk to librarians about seven book titles. This chart helped me to figure which ones of my books would be most interesting to many of their patrons.

	genre	target group	demand	featured in media	
NAKED TEXT Email Writing Skills for Teenagers	biz	students, teachers, parents	YES - students are often short on cash, teachers want to check out content	no - but NICHE book	Y
NAKED WORDS 2.0 The Effective 157-Word Email	biz	biz people, job seekers	YES - small business owners may not want to buy or check out content before they buy	SUCCESS magazine, BB's podcast, dozens of blogs	Y
NAKED TRUTHS About Getting Book Reviews	indie authors	indie authors	YES - many indie author groups meet at libraries	dozens of author blogs	Y
Naked News for Indie Authors How NOT to Invest Your Marketing $$$	indie authors	indie authors		a few author blogs	Y
NAKED TRUTHS About Getting Product Reviews on Amazon.com: 7 Insider tips to boost Sales	biz	biz people	NO – Business owners buy biz/ reference books	3. European business publications	X
Naked Eye-Opener To Reach the Dream You Must Forget About It	life skills	life skills	×	no	X
Naked Determination: 41 Stories About Overcoming Fear	life skills	life skills	×	Wilmington Star, dozens of blogs incl. Indian blogs	X

Learn How to Impress Librarians

Previously, I stated that one of the things that will help you in selling books to public libraries is its media coverage because it is one way how library users find out about your book regardless of whether it was reviewed by Kirkus, or not.

To pick an obvious example: According to WorldCat, E.L. James' novel *Fifty Shades of Grey* (Pub Date: May 25, 2011) can be located in 847 libraries around the world.

Please note again that many libraries do not supply information to WorldCat because today many US states have their own systems; the book is most likely in many more collections.

Though a later edition of *Fifty Shades of Grey* (Pub Date: April 3rd, 2012) was reviewed by Kirkus, Julie Bosman's review of the book titled "Discreetly Digital, Erotic Novel Sets American Women Abuzz," was published in *The New York Times* already on March 9, 2012.

Kirkus posted their review online five months later on Aug. 3rd, 2012; it did not get featured in their print magazine.

This goes to show that media coverage matters, on multiple levels.

Public libraries not only collect books but also magazines, periodicals, and specific articles. Therefore, if you or your book is featured in a known publication, you already got your foot through the door of libraries.

The nicest thing about this process is that most often it happens without you having to do anything but getting the media coverage. Though not every article will be collected, most public libraries collect newspapers, known magazines and also *library newsletters*.

Search: gisela hausmann

Advanced Search

Catalog | **CatalogPlus** | Images

Results 1 - 14 of 14 for gisela hausmann

Sorted by Relevance | Date

Refine by:

Library Catalog (3)

EBSCO EDS (11)
  Full Text
  Peer Reviewed

− **Availability**
At the library
Online

− **Found In**
Author (3)

− **Format**
Magazines (4)
BOOK (3) ◄
News (2)

− **Collection**
All Adult (3)
Main Library (3)

− **Language**
English (18)

− **Place**
united states (2)
russia (1)

− **Tag**
authors
books -- sales & prices
booksellers & bookselling
bookstores
libraries
more >

− **Content Provider**
NewsBank (6)
Literature Resource Center (2)
Business Insights: Essentials (2)

Naked Determination is a collection of stories about fear
Paula Hrbacek

News | Panama City Examiner (FL), December 3, 2013 Pensacola Book Review Examiner, 2pp

Please log in to see more details

Gisela Hausmann's dream was to see the w... more

Full Text from NewsBank

Additional actions

Naked text : email writing skills for teenagers / Gisela Hausmann. / Gisela Hausmann
Hausmann, Gisela

BOOK | 2015

Available at Main Library Local Authors
(LOCAUTH 004.692 Hausmann) see all

Request it

Additional actions

Finding Room on the Shelf.
PALMER, ALEX

Periodical | Publishers Weekly; 10/26/2015, Vol. 262 Issue 43, p34-36, 3p

Please log in to see more details

more

PDF

Additional actions

Naked truths about getting book reviews / by Gisela Hausmann. / by Gisela Hausmann
Hausmann, Gisela

BOOK | 2015

Available at Main Library Local Authors (LOCAUTH 028.1 Hausmann)
see all

Request it

Additional actions

You da (email) man! A guide to concise, commanding communiques
Vinnedge, Mary

Periodical | Success, August, 2015, p12, 1 p.

Please log in to see more details

Gisela Hausmann, author of Naked Words: ... more

View record in Business Insights: Essentials

Additional actions

TIP: Contact a dozen libraries in your area and see if you can volunteer for an educational talk, a local author fair, or any kind of library event that will most likely be featured in libraries' newsletters. Most libraries mention all relevant events because libraries want to attract different types of patrons. Consequently, being a guest at a library event is one of the easiest ways to get media coverage that will be listed in library catalogs.

Maybe, your name and book are already featured in your local library's catalog. Be sure to search in the CatalogPlus or Periodicals section of the online catalog. (Please see preceding illustration).

If you don't have any entries yet, or just one or two, pursue the media and try to get featured.

Here is a visual summary of the relatively easy to acquire options:

It is important to know that not every library collects the same content automatically. In other words, if you wrote a historic novel which was reviewed in a publication, this catalog entry will only be found in library systems of libraries whose collections hold a lot of historic novels.

Also, if you penned that novel while living in another city, the entry may be featured in that city's library system but not in the library system of the city where you live now. To find out which library system features this entry, you may have to scan multiple library systems.

TIP: Make sure that you collect all noteworthy entries so you can put together your own information sheet which you can use to prove existing media coverage when communicating with librarians.

If you know that you have been featured in print media but for some reason this information is not listed in your library's catalog, make a copy of each print article and the publication's title page, staple them together, and bring all of them with your book to your local library.

Entice the librarian to add the print media articles to their catalog by also offering to donate a copy of your book. As soon as the information is featured in only one public library's catalog, other libraries have access to it, too. This will help in getting your book in other libraries.

In the future when you approach librarians, always email a scan, send a print-out, or bring in person a copy of your author CatalogPlus sheet that features your book's media coverage. Librarians are busy people, therefore it helps if do the homework for them.

Please note: Because libraries are busy places with a limited number of employees, it will take time until your books as well as any print media coverage is added to their catalog and possibly to WorldCat.org; typically between 3 weeks and 3 months.

Your only option is to wait and monitor the library's website as often as you see fit.

Once your book is listed in one or more libraries – Help spread the word by doing some PR!

You can tell friends in person and you can also tweet about it. Help patrons find you and your book.

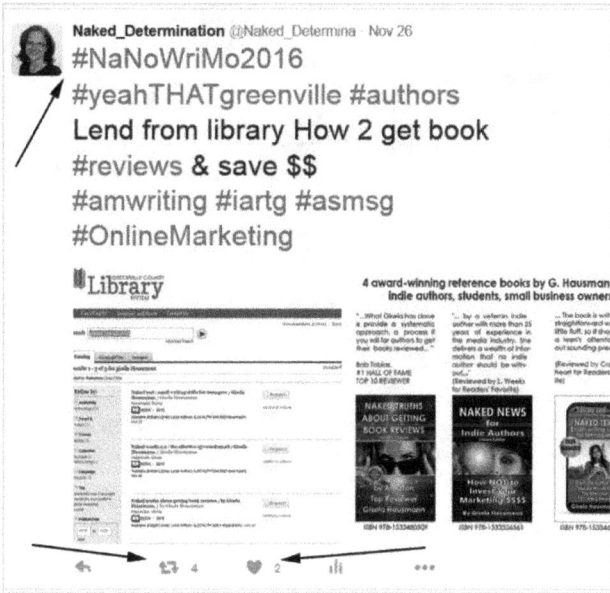

You'll be surprised how many Twitter users re-tweet library news.

You can also promote your book on Facebook this way. Surely, you have lots of friends who don't want to buy every book they see; why not give them an opportunity to read your book free? Your friends might even review it.

It's another way to promote your book and to nurture the funnel.

Gisela Hausmann
4 hrs · Independence · 🔔 ▼

Authors friends:
My book about "how to get book reviews" and "how to save marketing $$$" can be found in the following libraries;
• Greenville, SC
• Pickens County, SC
• Hendersonville, NC
• Fletcher, NC
• Key Largo, FL
• Livingston, LA
• Los Alamos, NM
and 2 college libraries in IA and VT, which you may not be able to visit.

Monitor How Your Book is Doing in Libraries

The provided example shows that my local library carries three of my books and one is rented out. There is even a waiting list: "1 hold on first copy returned of 1 copy." – Tweeting library news works!

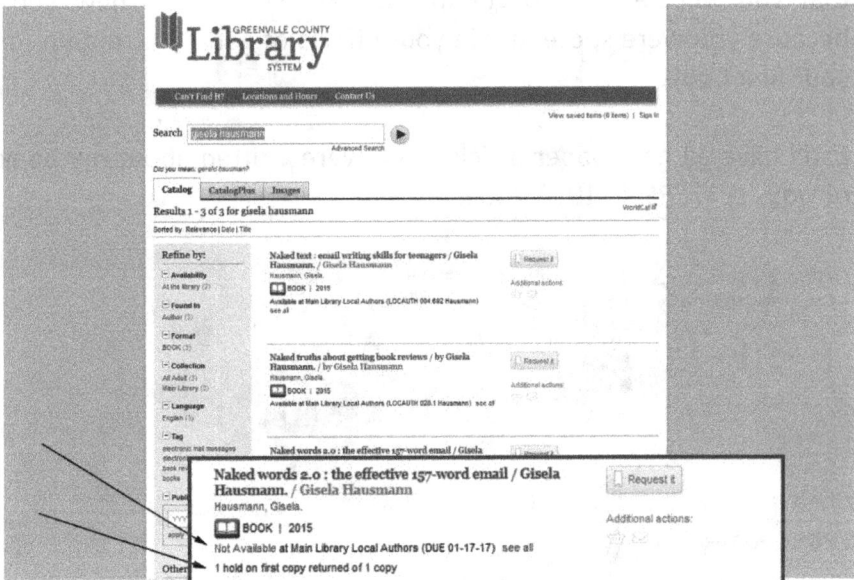

Why should you monitor if your book gets rented out?

If you see lots of demand, you may be able to talk your library into buying a second copy. If you also keep records of how often readers ask for your book, you might be able to convince libraries in surrounding counties to also buy a copy.

Additionally, you may be able to convince your library that they should invite you for a book reading, which – you guessed it – will be announced in the library's newsletter. With a bit of luck you may even be able to convince your local newspaper to cover such an event because it is a local event. In short, you could end up getting two more items of press coverage that you can reuse – to sell more books to more libraries.

TIP: Depending on the length of your book, you only need to check your book's availability in libraries every one to two weeks.

TIP: Always scan all newspaper clips and newsletters for your portfolio; you never know when you might need it. For instance when you release a new book, you could use these items to prove that you will be able to get media coverage for the new book because you were successful in your efforts of getting attention for your first book.

I still have all newspaper articles that were written about my book *obvious LETTERS*, in 1998-2000.

Create a Newsroom on Your Website

... to make it as easy as possible for librarians to see that you are promoting your book and that therefore patrons will ask for it.

GISELA HAUSMANN

One More Tip

If you checked out a few different books on WorldCat, undoubtedly, you have noticed that Amazon and Barnes & Noble aren't the only "Buy It"-sources listed. There is also BetterWorldBooks.com.

BetterWorldBooks.com is an organization that supports leading literacy initiatives around the world.

This illustration shows a part of WorldCat's listing of John Grisham's book "The Client" and below it the "Buy It"-section of an indie author's book.

Indie author book

If you want your book's listing to look like John Grisham's book (with more buying options), you could donate any number of books to this organization.

Please note, BetterWorldBooks.com will *not* add your book to WorldCat.org; only librarians and distributors can do that.

However, if your book is already listed on WorldCat, because a librarian added the listing, they will add their organization as a buying option. In short, your book could look just like John Grisham's famous legal thriller if you decide to donate any number of books.

Awards

Another huge topic is whether authors should enter their books in award competitions, or not. Once, I saw a remark in an online discussion forum which stated, "Authors who won an award think that awards matter, that winning helped them. The ones who didn't win say awards are not important."

That is a limiting view and I'll explain why, later.

Entering a book award costs about $75 per entry. Some (inexperienced) authors think that this means "authors can buy their way into becoming an award-winning author."

It is a ridiculous idea. Here is why:

- Every administrative effort costs money. Definitely, all authors want somebody to keep track of which judges received which books and their scores, and other related tasks.
- Though nobody really knows exact numbers, authors can expect about 800 to 1,500 books to be entered in each award, which implies that keeping track of all books and judges' scores requires a lot of administrative effort.

In short, you cannot buy your way into becoming an award-winning author. But, you can see "spending $75" as the fee for a class in "how your book stacks up against the competition." Though you can do the "course work" as described in this book for free and never enter your book, all of us know that our level of commitment rises with the amount of money at stake.

Think about it: If you buy a paid book review from Kirkus, you spend $425 on getting a 250-word retelling of your book's content, which for me did not even end up with good recap of my books' content. You also get a what I call the "verdict sentence," which may not be very telling.

My book *Naked Determination* was "judged"

> "A unique life well-lived, but the telling isn't quite ready for prime time." – *Kirkus Reviews*

The same book won two awards, one in each competition I entered the book.

TIP: I do not believe in entering a book in every award competition where it might score. To me, investing an additional $450 in entry fees ($75 x 6 entries) does not seem to add significant value. If you make about one dollar on the sale of one ebook, ask yourself if entering (and hopefully winning) additional awards will lead to an additional 450 sales that would not have happened had your book won only 1 or 2 awards?

There is really nothing to be learned from that my book *Naked Determination* won two awards but did not receive a favorable review from Kirkus, because my book *NAKED TEXT Email Writing Skills for Teenagers* also won two awards and did receive a favorable review from Kirkus.

However, you must ask yourself – Which kind of investment is going to benefit your book the most?

If you spend anywhere from $295 to $425 on a paid review you get a **chance** to use the "purchased goods (the review)" to sell books to public libraries.

On the other hand, if you see the $75 entry fee for an award as a "fee for taking a course" in making your book the best it can be, you may win more. But, make no mistake – YOU have to do the "course work" and learn the lessons, just like in college.

Here is one path to doing that.

First, examine awards and award categories and evaluate which one is the one that fits your book the most.

Two years ago, a friend of mine, a female African American entrepreneur, asked me if I believed that she should enter her business book in the *Readers Favorite Awards*, category "Nonfiction-Business," and if I thought that her book had a chance of winning.

I advised her to not limit herself to this one option but to also check out the *Reader Favorite Awards'* categories "Nonfiction Self Help" and "Nonfiction Women," because her book fit into these categories as well.

She should also check out other awards.

The *National Indie Excellence Awards* offer the categories
- "African American Non-Fiction",
- "Business-Entrepreneurship & Small Business",
- "Business-General," and
- "Business-Motivational."

The *International Book Awards* offer the categories
- "Business-Careers",
- "Business-Communications/Public Relations",
- "Business-Entrepreneurship & Small Business," and
- "Business- Management & Leadership."

And, that's just a few of the options she had. The variety of options may be similar for your book.

The next step is to inspect the list of past winners, check them out on Amazon and read at least the sample of each book. With a bit of luck, the one or other book may even be offered for free or on sale for 99 cents and you could buy the book to examine it more closely.

If you engage in these kind of activities, in other words, "take the course in learning how your book stacks up against the competition," you are going to WIN something: You will learn how good your book really is, and you'll have a better grasp on how it might fare.

That's because you will notice differences between the winners of different awards and different categories. For instance, while my friend's book might look "too specific" for the *Readers Favorite Award's* general category "Nonfiction-Business," it might be a perfect fit for the *National Indie Excellence Awards'* category "African American Non-Fiction" or "Business-Motivational." It might be an even better fit for entering the *International Book Awards'* category "Business – Management & Leadership."

In reality, many books do not win because their authors do not do this kind of research. The juries' hands are tied. They can only select winners that fit perfectly into a specific category.

Please know that all my recommendations are thoroughly tested. My books won the following book awards:

2016 Honorary Mention **Readers' Favorite** Awards
2016 **International Book** Awards Finalist
2016 **National Indie** Excellence Awards Finalist
2015 **Kindle Book** Awards Finalist
2014 Gold **Readers' Favorite** Award
2013 Bronze **eLit** Awards

Also, I do not enter all my books in awards; after all there is no superlative to multi-award winning author. Once your books have won two awards you are a multi-award winning author.

Remember the quote I listed in the beginning of this chapter:

"Authors who won an award think that awards matter, that winning them helped them. The ones who didn't win say awards are not important."

It seems to me that the person who stated this thinks of entering a book in an award competition like of buying a lottery ticket: Maybe you'll win, and maybe – not.

The truth is, if you do the research, you will most certainly become a better author and you will also significantly increase your odds of winning.

Additionally, do not limit yourself to only entering your book in book award competitions. There is probably a lot more you can do.

Since I am an email evangelist who wrote a pretty cool book about writing best emails, I entered the SparkyAward 2016, specifically the category "Best Subject Line." It is awarded by Spark Post, the company that sends out twenty-five percent of all legitimate emails, worldwide, in other words – an industry leader.

I truly believe in the power of email as a tool, applied myself fully, and won this award.

Winning an **industry award** means that you have skin in the game, you are all in, you didn't stop at writing your book, you live and breathe your field of expertise!

If, for instance, you own a pet hotel and you also write cat and/or dog stories, surely, potential buyers of your book would be impressed to read that you are, for instance, "author xyz, winner of the Best Pet Hotel Award."

Some other awards (of the hundreds of options):

- National Geographic *Travel* Photographer of the Year
- National Geographic *Nature* Photographer of the Year
http://travel.nationalgeographic.com/

- Comedy Wildlife Photography Awards
http://www.comedywildlifephoto.com

Various Costume Awards in many US states and other countries
- Historical Masquerade
- Sci-Fi & Fantasy Masquerade
- Hall Costume Awards

There are also awards for the best social media presence:
- Facebook Presence
- Instagram Presence
- Periscope Presence
- Snapchat Presence
- Tumblr Presence
- Twitter Presence
- YouTube Presence
- Regional awards
- Content and Media
- Mobile Sites & Apps
- Strategy & Engagement
http://shortyawards.com/

You are into Sci-Fi? Maybe you invented a gizmo that is also mentioned in your book(s)?
http://www.popsci.com/tags/invention-awards

Lastly, there are also blogger awards, from best picture blog awards to podcast blog awards; a search on Google will reveal the many options.

Take Action

The most important part of creating a marketing funnel is to – Take Action!

If you don't take action, nothing is going to happen. It's that simple. Here is a true story that illustrates what can happen when you do.

Aside from *NAKED TRUTHS About Getting Book Reviews,* I also penned *NAKED TRUTHS About Getting Product Reviews on Amazon.com: 7 Insider tips to boost Sales.*

It's a business book. Though I really wanted to enter this book in an award competition, I felt that entering the book in just any award competition (category: Business) just didn't make sense. The book could only gain recognition in business people's circles if it would win a *designated* business book award.

There was only one problem with this: The most reputable US business book award, the Axiom Award, is being awarded by the Jenkins Group, who – charges winners for winning.

I do not support that concept.

Undoubtedly, designing an award is the a pre-requisite to holding an award competition, thus its costs should be covered by the entry fees. Winning an award is not some additional task or activity; it is the goal of the event. Why "punish" the winners by charging them an additional fee* up to $130 to actually receive their digital award seals?

> [*To my knowledge, the Jenkins Group (eLit Awards, Illumination Awards, IPPY Awards, Moonbeam Awards, Axiom Awards) is the only organization that charges winners for digital award seals.]

Though I would defend this, my position, and argue it in any forum, of course this didn't help me, because if I did not enter my book in the award competition, it could not possibly win.

Caught between a rock and a hard place, I searched for other designated business book awards and discovered the *800-CEO Award*. Most surprisingly, entering this award was free. The cut-off date was September 30. I immediately shipped two copies of my book and was very happy.

Unfortunately, this happiness lasted only for a few days. On October 3, 2016, totally unexpectedly, Amazon changed its Community Guidelines for posting reviews, thereby making quite a bit of my book's content obsolete.

Even if my book won, it would be meaningless because I could not sell the book as it was any longer; it featured outdated content. Under the influence of a pitcher of coffee, I devised a plan. I would rewrite my book immediately and present new solutions in accordance with Amazon's changed guidelines. I also alerted my editor that she needed to edit these corrected chapters as soon as I could deliver them, or all my efforts would be useless.

For three days, I did nothing but create new solutions for Amazon vendors and rewrite the chapters that had to be fixed.

Only one week after Amazon had turned the world of millions of their vendors upside down, and also my world as an expert author, I was able to email the 800-CEO Award Committee, asking if I could submit the corrected edition.

To cut this short, my book did not win an 800-CEO Award. However, while I was pondering solutions for Amazon vendors' quests to get product reviews, I realized that I was probably the first person to address this new development. This situation was an obvious opportunity for media coverage.

Once I had finished updating my book, I searched for names of editors who write about "Amazon, Amazon product vendors, and related topics." The most outstanding journalist was Bloomberg's Spencer Soper, who writes most insightful articles about anything related to selling merchandise on Amazon. So, I wrote him an email. Even though I am an award-winning email evangelist, I wrote, edited, and re-wrote my email; considering Bloomberg's status, it had to be the best email it could be.

Three days later, when I still had not heard from Mr. Soper, I called him. Though I was prepared to very cautiously and politely explain why I called, he recognized me by my one-sentence-mini-introduction and said, "Oh yes! I read your email. **You also wrote a book about this topic, right?**"

And, that's how my book ended up getting featured in a podcast on Bloomberg.

If a week earlier I would have found the magic bottle and the genie would have said to me, "Pick one: Winning the Axiom Award, winning the 800-CEO Award, or Getting featured on Bloomberg!" I would have picked Bloomberg.

But, that's not how life happens. In reality, getting what you want means trying to do your best, looking for best solutions, and NOT GIVING UP. – It works!

So, TAKE ACTION! Though hundreds, if not thousands, of author marketing services will tell you that if you only pay them for this or that task, they will help you to get

- print media coverage,
- one or more guest appearances on TV,
- sales to public libraries,

chances are – YOU are your work's best advocate.

Don't believe that? Just think about it: Do you believe that any publicist could have figured out that this very moment when Amazon changed its user guidelines was the best moment to pitch Bloomberg? And, if a publicist would have come up with this idea, how much would I have had to pay them?

1,000 dollars?

2,000?

3,000?

Though I don't know which one of these numbers you picked, imagine now that an author friend of yours who writes the same genre as you do will pay you this amount if you can get him media coverage for his book.

How much effort would you put in finding the right publication and putting together the perfect pitch?

That's the mindset, and – you can do this for your own book!

ADDENDUM - Additional Resources

100 Pitches to Help You Brainstorm

This list of pitches features suggestions to inspire you to come up with your own ideas. Every part is interchangeable. If you can't come up with seven ideas/solutions/ways, simply pitch five ideas or three. Reading all 100 pitches from all genres will help you to brainstorm best.

Children's

1. 5 books parents should read to their child to prepare them for starting school

2. *(Anniversaries of July 22, 2013):* Prince George is already a pop culture icon. 5 books about princes (or princesses) that your child will love

3. March 3 is *Dr. Seuss birthday.* Does your local library/ children's museum/ city host a "Seuss Fest" to encourage children to read? 3 reasons why parents should go

4. *Take Your Daughter to Work Day* – 7 ideas to help you prepare so your daughter will love your workplace

5. March 16th is *"Absolutely Incredible Kids Day,"* the day when parents are supposed to write a letter to their child to show kids they are loved and cared for. Local children's book author has 5 tips on what you could write

6. *(Halloween's Day)* Are you worried about little trick-and-treaters' teeth? Local author shares 5 creative ideas on what to give instead.

7. *(Valentine's Day)* Are you worried that your child will eat too much candy? Local author will share 5 creative ideas what to give instead.

Cook books

8.   *Mother's Days* is known for having the strongest restaurant sales. Should you take out your mom for brunch, lunch, or cook yourself? Local cook book author shares insights

9.   Are you worried about gaining weight over the holidays? 9 delicious, healthy side dishes that are easy to prepare

10.   May 4, 2017 is *National Orange Juice Day*. Local cookbook author shares 7 delicious recipes to cook with orange juice

11.   Do you feel stressed out on *Thanksgiving*? Local cookbook author gives tips to make the most of your kitchen space

12.   April 26th is *National Pretzel Day*. Did you know that Pretzels are believed to be the world's oldest snack? Local cook book authors shares 5 tips to bake the best home-made pretzels

13.   March 1 is *Peanut Butter Lovers' Day*. 7 Ways to make a peanut butter sandwich your child will love

14.   March 14th is *National Potato Chip Day*. Local cook book author shares 8 Party-Perfect Potato Chip Dishes

Historic Novels

15.   *Fat Tuesday* – Why some cities celebrate it! Plus, The Best parties in town

16.   (June 10th) The Anniversary of the publication of Gone With the Wind is coming up. Why are people still fascinated with historic novels about the South and will always be!

17.   *Leap Day* – 5 myths and tradition (e.g. women propose to their men) you need to know so you won't get caught off-guard

18. *International Women's Day* (March 8) – 5 books about remarkable women you and your daughters should read

19. March 17th is *Saint Patrick's Day*. 5 Favorite Sayings to make your coworkers' day!

20. (1 July 2017) Twenty years ago, Great Britain transferred sovereignty over Hong Kong to the People's Republic of China. – Is it a coincidence that historic novels about the city often become bestsellers? *[Tai-Pan by James Clavell, Noble House by James Clavell, Kowloon Tong by Paul Theroux, The Piano Teacher by Janice Y.K. Lee, The Language of Threads by Gail Tsukiyama]*

21. The *Anniversary of the Sinking of the Titanic* (14 April 1912) is coming up. Did you know there are 7 "titanic museums"? Why are we so much more fascinated with this particular disaster than with others? Local author can explain.
    [Titanic Museum Branson, MO, Titanic Historical Society, Indian Orchard, MA, Titanic Experience, Orlando, FL, Titanic Museum, Pigeon Forge, TN, Titanic Museum, Southampton, Titanic Museum Belfast, Maritime Museum, Halifax Nova Scotia]

Horror

22. 3 Ways to be lucky on *Friday the 13th*

23. 7 haunted houses in ... (local area)... you want to visit this Halloween

24. 5 super-easy, delicious snacks for your Halloween Party

25. 7 Tricks to decorate your house for *Halloween* – for under 50 bucks

26. On May 26, 2017 Bram Stoker's "Dracula" will be 120 years old. 3 Trivia facts to impress your co-workers

27. January 28, 2017 – Stephen King's novel "Shining" will be 40 years old. 7 facts about Stephen King novels you probably did not know.

28. *(for horror authors who live in Colorado)* January 28, 2017 – Stephen King's novel "Shining" will be 40 years old. Are you planning a trip to the Stanley Hotel in Estes Park, Colorado? Local horror writer offers tips

Nonfiction (Create pitches based on your expertise)

29. 3 Tips for Email Networking

30. Only 1 in 9 South Carolina 11th graders is "ready" for success in college, statistics say => One of the most important skills teenagers need to succeed...

31. The drought in California is getting worse. What vegetables should you plant to save $25 of your grocery bill every week?

32. Why you should take at least 5 pictures of your mom every *Mother's Day*!

33. Planning your *4th of July* party? 3 Tricks to do the cooking in half the time!

34. Do you bring your accountant shoeboxes full of receipts? – 7 Tips to stay organized before *Tax Day* arrives

35. Want to have the greenest lawn on the block? 3 Simple things to do this spring for a super green lawn all summer long

Romance

36. 7 sweet gestures your spouse will appreciate more than chocolates and flowers

37. Have a *Valentine's* picnic! – 5 truly romantic spots less than one hour of … (your city/region) …

38. 3 historic practices celebrating *Valentine's* during the days of yore that you have never heard of…

39. How to celebrate *Valentine's* with the kids; and still find time to be "romantic"?

40. April 2 is *Reconciliation Day. (Newspaper columnist Ann Landers promoted in 1989.)* Local romance author gives tips on what to say if you want to reconcile but don't know "how" to say it

41. June is the most popular months for weddings. Local romance author shares 7 tips to plan a wedding most effectively

42. (May 2017) Pippa Middleton will be getting married. In stark contrast to her famous sister Kate, Pippa will get married in a small church. Will she set a new trend?

Humor/Satire

43. *April Fool's Day* – Local humorist and funny book author advises about the do's and don'ts of workplace pranks

44. January 3: It's *Fruitcake Toss Day*. Have you tossed yours? If not, you must store it until next Christmas. 3 locations where you could toss the cake

45. 7 Fabulous *April's Fool Day* Pranks for the Office

46. April 7th is *"National Beer Day."* 3 facts about beer AND 3 safety tips

47. April 30th is *Hairstyle Appreciation Day*. 3 Tips to shine… (pause)… for MEN!

48.   August 18th is *Bad Poetry Day*. Local author recites 3 really awful poems to start your day on a funny note!

49.   Oktoberfest 2017: (September 23 – October 8) Local humorist offers tips on what to drink, what to eat, and what jokes to tell when visiting one of the fests.

Sci-fi

50.   July 8, 2017 – The 70th anniversary of the "Roswell"-incident is coming up. Do you believe in UFOs or aliens? Local Sci-Fi author and expert shares what to expect when visiting the Roswell UFO Festival 2017 in Roswell, NM | Everfest

51.   July 8th is *"Roswell Day."* – UFO-Festivals in the United States (or specific region) and why you should attend

52.   July 8, 2017 – The 70th Anniversary of the "Roswell"-incident is coming up. Want to throw a UFO Alien Party?

53.   May 4th is *"Star Wars Day."* – Star Wars Festivals in the United States (or specific region) and why you should attend

54.   NASA Launch Day (pls see schedule https://www.nasa.gov/launchschedule) – Why does this mission matter to all of us? Local Sci-Fi author can explain

55.   "... movie..." will open this weekend. Why Sci-Fi and dystopian stories are more popular than ever

56.   (July 20, 2019) It's the 50th anniversary of the Moon Landing. 5 gadgets mentioned in Sci-Fi novels we use today in our everyday life

Self-help

57.   Don't want to be alone in 2017? Local romance author reveals 5 unusual locations to meet people "accidentally"

58.   (fourth Sunday in October) *Mother-In-Law Day* is coming up. Local self-help author offers 5 tips on what to do to become the favorite son/daughter-in-law

59.   Do you know that 3 out of 4 people fail to keep their New Year's resolutions? Three simple tricks that will help you to stay motivated

60.   Traveling with kids during the holidays? 7 Tips to keep the little ones in your life entertained in the car or on the plane

61.   *Valentine's* is coming up! 7 Tips to pull off a perfect first date

62.   Are you concerned about America's drug epidemic? 3 warning signs you must know

63.   Local self-help expert shares 7 Tips on "How to write a bucket list"

Business

64.   *No Socks Day* is on May 8th. Set a new trend at your company and look like a team builder. Local author tells you how

65.   September 6 is *Read a Book Day*. Start a business book club at your office. Local author recommends 5 books to get you started.

66.   Major cyber attacks are reported on a monthly basis: 9 relatively easy to-do steps for small business owners to prevent a cyber attack

67.   Last Saturday in November is *Small Business Saturday*. 5 Tips to market your small business on social media platforms

68.   Small business owners: Do you market on social media platforms? 5 effective ways to market to locals

69. Why 2017 is a great time to start a business in (state)

70. It's graduation time! 5 Tips to write an outstanding "New Grad"-resume

Health

71. *World Health Day* is on April 7th. Five easy things you should do right now to be in the shape of your life by the end of the year

72. *National Stress Awareness Day* is on April 16th. Three high stress level indicators you need to know

73. *National Stress Awareness Day* is on April 16th. Seven tiny changes everybody can make to reduce stress in their lives

74. Spring is coming up. Explore these three hiking routes (city parks)

75. Winter is coming: Fitness expert recommends 7 exercises you can do at home if it's too cold to be outside

76. Do your New Year's resolutions include losing weight? Local expert author reveals 5 apps that can help you stay on target

77. Vacation time is coming up! 7 things you should check when booking a hotel online

Sports

78. Is your husband or boyfriend a football fan but you are not? Local author presents a cheat sheet: 5 Super Bowl facts to mention so you'll look like a pro

79. Christmas and the holidays are the season of giving. – 5 local charities where you can volunteer

80. Super Bowl weekend: According to the National Chicken Council, Americans will eat more than 1.3 billion wings. What to serve if you expect guests who are vegans or vegetarians.

81. The 2018 Winter Olympics will feature 4 four new events. What you need to know about Snowboarding big air, Curling mixed doubles, Speed skating mass start, and Alpine skiing team event.

82. Tailgating parties as a way to build community and support for local schools' sports' programs and teams. What you can do to help

83. Like Sports? 5 Local events that are worth visiting.

More pitches

84. September 8th is *International Literacy Day*. A group of local authors are holding an author fair. Meet them and their books. X percent of the proceeds go to (local charity)

85. *Father's Day* is coming up. Worldwide, people spend around $12.7 billion dollars on ties and neck wear. Local adventure book author explains the pluses and minuses of buying this traditional gift

86. April 27th is *Tell a Story Day*. 9 Books your teenager will love

87. Drones are getting more popular. Should you think about making/delivering orders via drones in the next year/near future?

88. April 22, 2017 is *Earth Day*. Attend an event OR throw your own "plant a tree"-event

89. Always wanted to run a marathon? Try a half marathon first.

90. Christmas is coming up. 5 Unusual gift ideas for the fitness fan in your life

91. Hurricane season is coming up. Local author who lived through hurricane .... to tell the tale shares tips you don't want to miss

92. September 9th is *Teddy Bear Day*. Local children's book author recommends 9 bear-books to read with your child

93. September 22nd is *Hobbit Day* (birthday of Frodo and Bilbo) - 5 Ways to celebrate the day – from a marathon movie session to throwing your own Hobbit party

94. Consumers are getting ready to shop: Business book author shares 5 marketing ideas How to boost Your *Black Friday Sales*

95. March 25th is *Tolkien Reading Day*. Local fantasy author shares insights on how reading fantasy books can hook your teen on reading

96. *(Father's Day)* Does your dad really need another tie? Home-improvement expert shares 5 great gift ideas for the dad who has everything (including too many ties)

97. Another "strange/unexplained environmental occurrence (e.g. Siberian mystery craters)!" – Are you worried? Local author of dystopian novels and prepper books advises 3 minimal action steps to be prepared for most emergency situations

98. Christmas is coming – 3 Tips to teach your child about giving

99. The holiday season is approaching rapidly. Business book author explains how to promote your business with holiday greetings and marketing

100. Earth Day's 50th anniversary in 2020. More than a billion people worldwide will be involved. Local expert tells what's happening in our area.

Action Steps

☐ Have at least 3 reviews on Goodreads (WorldCat.org shows 3 reviews on each book's main page)

☐ Decide if you want to reply to journalists' queries via HARO or choose and pitch the publications you want your books to be seen in; to succeed faster – do both!

☐ Subscribe to HARO – right now!

☐ Make it a habit to scan HARO's emails at least 4 times/week

☐ Respond to every HARO query you can pitch well

☐ Choose publications you want your book to be featured in (Check out magazines at your local bookstore or use the list of websites in this book's addendum)

☐ Write down the 3 top publications you want your book to be featured in:

☐ _____

☐ _____

☐ _____

☐ Look for the names of journalists and bloggers you want to pitch

☐ Follow them on Twitter

☐ Read a few of their articles and comment in the comment section

☐ Make it a habit to tweet/share these journalists' articles regularly

- ☐ Create 3 best pitches. (You can "reuse" them until they get featured in a publication)
- ☐ Depending on how fast you want to succeed, pitch three journalists or bloggers per day, per week or per month
- ☐ Make it a habit to monitor your media coverage every day
- ☐ As soon as you get featured, prepare tweets and tweet them regularly
- ☐ Create your own list of hashtags to attract new followers
- ☐ Create a newsroom on your website *before* you contact any library
- ☐ Make sure your book is in your local library's collection (if need be – donate it); you want your book in your local library's collection before you try to sell it to others
- ☐ Decide if you want to contact libraries via phone, email, or mail
- ☐ Create a contact list that lists the names, phone numbers and (email) addresses of librarians you want to contact
- ☐ Inquire about printing costs if you want to send librarians postcards or letters
- ☐ If you decide to go that route have fun and design an eye-catching mailing
- ☐ Be sure to mention your newsroom's URL on the postcard or in the letter
- ☐ Monitor WorldCat and state libraries' websites
- ☐ Tweet your library news!

Two Dozen Websites Every Author Needs to Know

Lists of public libraries by US state:
http://www.publiclibraries.com/**alabama**.htm

||||

48 states

||||

http://www.publiclibraries.com/**wyoming**.htm

List of the largest libraries in the United States
https://en.wikipedia.org/wiki/List_of_the_largest_libraries_in_the_United_States

State Library Systems
Some states have their own library catalog systems, instead of using WorldCat.

C/W MARS (Central and Western Massachusetts, 155 libraries)
http://www.cwmars.org/

Evergreen Indiana (State of Indiana - 112 libraries)
https://evergreen.lib.in.us

GA Pines (State of Georgia- 282 libraries)
https://gapines.org/eg/opac/home

King County Library System (Washington, 50 libraries)
http://kcls.org/catalog

MaineCat (Maine, 100 library collections)
http://mainecat.maine.edu/

Missouri Evergreen (29 Libraries)
http://missourievergreen.org/eg/opac/home

NC Cardinal (State of North Carolina - 93 libraries)
http://nccardinal.org

New York Public Library (NYPL) (NYC - 87 branches)
https://www.nypl.org/collections

Sage Library System (Northeast Oregon, 60 libraries)
https://sagelib.org/

South Dakota Libraries Network (61 libraries)
http://www.sdln.net/staff/members.php

2017 Best Liberal Arts Colleges (college libraries)
http://www.usnews.com/education/best-colleges/articles/slideshows/us-news-best-liberal-arts-colleges

Reach Out and Read! - Donate books to Children's Hospitals
http://www.nationwidechildrens.org/reach-out-and-read-giving

Research Data about libraries
http://www.pewinternet.org/search/?query=libraries

MeetUp Writers' Groups
https://www.meetup.com/find/writing/

Indie Author Day Events
http://indieauthorday.com/where/

Indie Author Day: Get Involved!
http://self-e.libraryjournal.com/indieauthorday/

US Writing Conferences & Events (sorted by US -states)
http://www.newpages.com/writers-resources/writing-conferences-events

2016-2017 Bizarre, Wacky and Unique Holidays (list of days perfect for pitching TV-anchors)
http://www.holidayinsights.com/moreholidays/

List of US newspapers by state
http://www.usnpl.com/

List of US TV-stations by state
http://www.usnpl.com/index_tv.php

List of magazines by circulation (worldwide)
https://en.wikipedia.org/wiki/List_of_magazines_by_circulation

The world's 50 most powerful blogs
https://www.theguardian.com/technology/2008/mar/09/blogs

Book Awards
https://www.goodreads.com/award

~~~~~~~~~~~~~~~~~~~~~~~~~~~~~~~~~~*~*~*~~~~~~~~~~~~~~~~~~~~~~~~~~~~~

My company Educ-Easy Books sells mailing lists / address labels of public libraries in many US states. For more information please go to: http://www.giselahausmann.com/author_services.html

~~~~~~~~~~~~~~~~~~~~~~~~~~~~~~*~*~*~~~~~~~~~~~~~~~~~~~~~~~~~~~~

Getting your book in public libraries:

Media coverage:

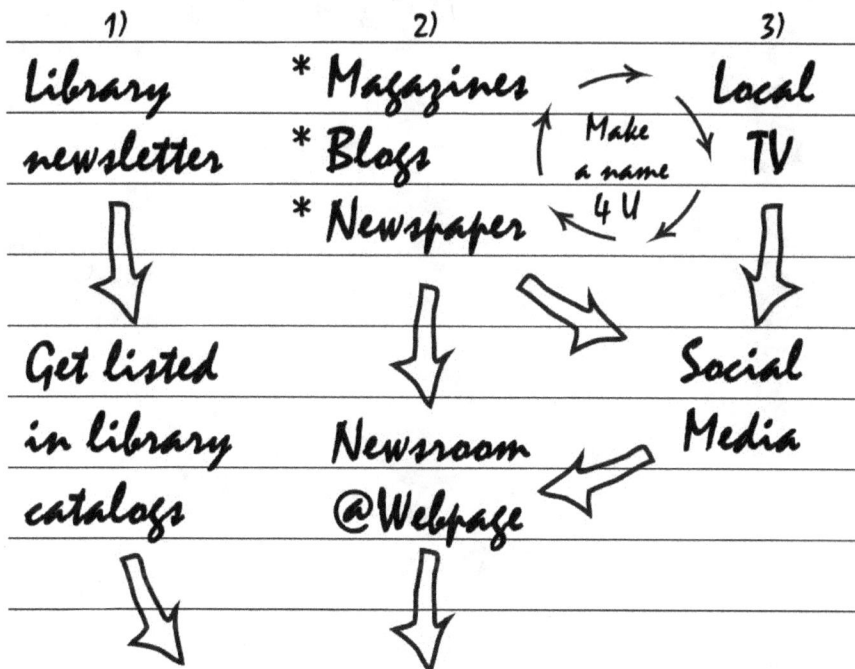

1)	2)	3)
Library newsletter	* Magazines * Blogs * Newspaper	Local TV

Make a name 4 U

↓ (from Library newsletter)

Get listed in library catalogs

↓ (from Magazines/Blogs/Newspaper)

Newsroom @Webpage

Social Media

↓↓

Visit/ Call/ Email/ Snail Mail Libraries

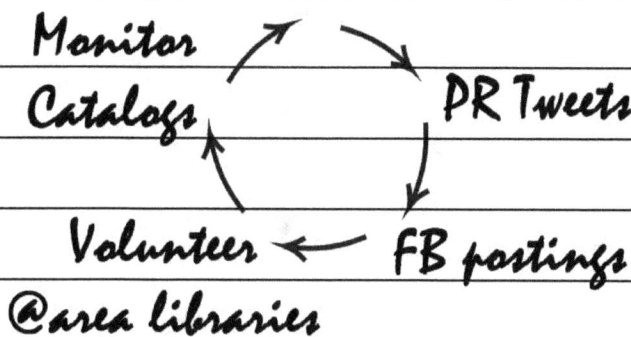

Monitor Catalogs → PR Tweets → FB postings → Volunteer @area libraries

Unique holidays for MY book's genre:

_____

_____

_____

_____

_____

_____

_____

_____

_____

_____

_____

_____

_____

_____

_____

_____

_____

_____

_____

Brainstorm &
Spin off some ideas

.... Ways to ...

Brainstorm &
Spin off some ideas

.... Tips to ...

Brainstorm &
Spin off some ideas

.... Unusual Ideas ...

Contacts:

Hometown library:

College library:

Former hometown(s) & contacts:

Topics I could speak about @ library events:

_____

_____

_____

_____

_____

_____

_____

_____

_____

_____

_____

_____

_____

_____

_____

_____

_____

_____

CHECKLIST
Information that will help spark librarians' interest

MEDIA coverage
(ideally a link to online newsroom) ☐

Link to paid REVIEW(s) ☐

AWARDS(s) ☐

Is your book already listed
on WORLDCAT ? ☐

Info WHO SELLS your book
(Amazon, B&N, Baker & Taylor, ☐
Walmart etc.)

Some of the most active local US Goodreads Groups
(check off groups that sound interesting)

☐   Uniting Southeastern Authors

☐   Southern Belles and Beaus

☐   Book Nerds of Northeast Alabama

☐   Shoals Area Book Chicks (NW Alabama — NW Mississippi)

☐   Arizona Readers Club

☐   Arizona Goodreads Club

☐   Santa Barbara Book Club

☐   Future Teachers, Reading and Reading (California)

☐   Southern California Events

☐   California Southern University Book Club

☐   Sunnyvale Public Library (California)

☐   Pantsuit Nation Connecticut

☐   20s/30s Fort Myers book club (Florida)

☐   St. Pete FL Book Club (Florida)

☐   Volusia County Public Library (Florida)

☐   Middle Georgia Readers Guild

☐   Forsyth County Public Library (Georgia)

☐   Columbus GA book club

☐   The Greener Reader (Hawaii)

☐   Madison Library District Goodreads Seasonal Challenge (Idaho)

☐   Illinois State NSDAR Book Group

☐   Evanston Public Library Science Fiction & Fantasy Book Discussion Group (Illinois)

- ☐ ACPL Online Book Club (Indiana)
- ☐ Dubuque Virtual Book Club (Iowa)
- ☐ Burlington Iowa Public Library Book Clubs
- ☐ Kansas City Moms, Daughters, and Friends
- ☐ Together We Will Bluegrass Book Club (Kentucky)
- ☐ Next-door (Louisville) Book Club (Kentucky)
- ☐ Lexington Reads (Kentucky)
- ☐ Shreveport/Bossier Readers Club Louisiana
- ☐ Shreve Memorial Library (Louisiana)
- ☐ Charles County Public Library (Maryland)
- ☐ Nothing Like Hood Fiction from DMV Area! (DC, Maryland and Virginia)
- ☐ South Shore Readers (Massachusetts)
- ☐ Tyngsboro Book & Food Club (Massachusetts)
- ☐ Eat Your Words, Boston Book Club (Massachusetts)
- ☐ Henika District Library (Michigan)
- ☐ Minnesota Readers
- ☐ Pantsuit Nation Minnesota
- ☐ Mississippi Writers
- ☐ Book Lovers in Missouri
- ☐ Omaha Readers (Nebraska)
- ☐ NJ 20-Something's Book Club
- ☐ Jessica N.'s Yoga Book Club (New Jersey)
- ☐ The Online Book Cafe (New Jersey)
- ☐ NJ: Young Fantasy Reads Book Group

- ☐ Morris County Book Club Meetup (New Jersey)
- ☐ Liberté Book Club (New Jersey)
- ☐ The Book Club (New Jersey)
- ☐ Passaic Public Library (New Jersey)
- ☐ ~A Time Traveler's Guide to New York~
- ☐ Glens Falls (NY) Online Book Discussion Group
- ☐ Our Shared Shelf (NYC) —
- ☐ A Novel Idea: a NYC Bookclub
- ☐ New Yorkers
- ☐ Nordic Book Club (NYC)
- ☐ Rochester and Upstate New York
- ☐ Fayetteville Free Library Skype Book Club! (New York)
- ☐ Brooklyn Bookworms! (New York)
- ☐ Goodreads in North Carolina
- ☐ Charlotte Mecklenburg Library (North Carolina)
- ☐ North Vagolinians (North Carolina)
- ☐ North Carolina Urban Fiction
- ☐ Thrillers & Chillers (Ohio)
- ☐ Choose Your Own Adventure! (Ohio)
- ☐ Oregon to Utah - Nature Girls Unite!
- ☐ Fresh*Reads (Texas)
- ☐ HPL Reads Book Club — (Texas)
- ☐ Flower Mound Public Library (Texas)
- ☐ Dallas/Ft. Worth Readers Club (Texas)

- [ ] Children's Literature Association of Utah
- [ ] League of Vermont Writers
- [ ] Virginia Beach Book Club
- [ ] Better Than Starbucks (Virginia)
- [ ] NOVA Men's Book Group (Virginia)
- [ ] The Bloomsbury Group & Friends (Virginia)
- [ ] Read Wine (Virginia)
- [ ] NoVA Lit Chicks (Virginia)
- [ ] NELA Book Club(Washington)
- [ ] Hudson Area Public Library Book Talk (Wisconsin)
- [ ] The Novel Clique (Wisconsin)
- [ ] The Inquisitive Bibliophiles (Wisconsin)

Notes:

_____

_____

_____

_____

_____

_____

_____

_____

_____

_____

_____

_____

_____

_____

_____

_____

Notes:

Notes:

Notes:

THANK YOU for buying

BOOK MARKETING: The Funnel Factor
Including 100 Media Pitches

Please leave a review at Amazon.com – It helps authors
to find out what readers would like to read more of.

To find out about upcoming "naked (no-fluff) books"
please subscribe at

http://www.giselahausmann.com/free-creative-ideas.html

Please know that this author is an e-mail evangelist.
I value and respect subscribers and
will not inundate you with sales e-mails.

* * *

More books:

NAKED TRUTHS ABOUT GETTING PRODUCT REVIEWS ON AMAZON.COM

Reviews Reviews Reviews

7 INSIDER TIPS TO BOOST SALES

BY AMAZON TOP REVIEWER GISELA HAUSMANN

FULLY REVISED & UPDATED APRIL 2017

NAKED TRUTHS ABOUT GETTING BOOK REVIEWS 2018

4th EDITION

By Amazon Top Reviewer GISELA HAUSMANN

Book Marketing

The Funnel Factor

Includes 100 media pitches

by 28-year industry veteran Gisela Hausmann

NAKED GOOD READS

HOW TO FIND READERS

BY GISELA HAUSMANN

AUTHOR OF 'NAKED TRUTHS ABOUT GETTING BOOK REVIEWS' AND OT...

the Little
Blue Book
for Authors

**101 CLUES
TO GET MORE OUT
OF FACEBOOK**

Gisela Hausmann
award-winning Writer
of remakably naked, no-fluff Content

the Little
Blue Book
for Authors

53
DOs & DON'Ts
NOBODY
IS TELLING
YOU

:)

by Amazon Top Reviewer
GISELA HAUSMANN

NAKED TEXT
Email-writing skills
for teenagers

NIEA
FINALIST
NATIONAL INDIE
EXCELLENCE®
AWARDS

From the author of
"Naked Words 2.0
The Effective
157-Word Email"

Gisela Hausmann

NAKED WORDS 2.0
The Effective
157-Word Email

How to
get
your
emails
read
by
everyone

INTERNATIONAL
BOOK AWARDS
FINALIST

by **GISELA HAUSMANN**
Winner of the
2016 Sparky Award "Best Subject Line"

GISELA HAUSMANN

NAKED EYE-OPENER

TO REACH THE DREAM YOU MUST FORGET ABOUT IT

NAKED DETERMINATION

41 Stories About Overcoming Fear

Gisela Hausmann

Gisela Hausmann

How I Built Myself a Hobbit Fire Pit

EMAIL HUMOR

BAT SHIT CRAZY REVIEW REQUESTS

BY AMAZON TOP REVIEWER
GISELA HAUSMANN

About the Author

Gisela Hausmann is the winner of the

- 2016 Sparky Award "Best Subject Line" (industry award)
- 2017 IAN Book of the Year Awards Finalist
- 2016 International Book Awards Finalist
- 2016 National Indie Excellence Awards Finalist
- 2015 Kindle Book Awards Finalist
- 2014 Gold Readers' Favorite Award
- 2013 Bronze eLit Awards

Her work has been featured on Bloomberg (tech podcast) and on NBC News (biz blog), in *SUCCESS* and in *Entrepreneur*.

Born to be an adventurer, Gisela has co-piloted single-engine planes, produced movies, and worked in the industries of education, construction, and international transportation. Gisela's friends and fans know her as a woman who goes out to seek the unusual and rare adventure.

A unique mixture of wild risk-taker and careful planner, Gisela globe-trotted almost 100,000 kilometers on three continents, including to the locations of her favorite books: Doctor Zhivago's Russia, Heinrich Harrer's Tibet, and Genghis Khan's Mongolia.

Gisela Hausmann graduated with a Master's degree in Film & Mass Media from the University of Vienna. She now lives in Greenville, South Carolina.

To subscribe to Gisela's Blog pls subscribe at
http://www.giselahausmann.com/free-creative-ideas.html

Gisela's website: http://www.giselahausmann.com/
Follow her at https://twitter.com/Naked_Determina

www.ingramcontent.com/pod-product-compliance
Lightning Source LLC
Chambersburg PA
CBHW072251270326
41930CB00010B/2344